A
Larger
Hope

*Dedicated to those who long for a more vibrant faith,
a more inclusive church, and a more beautiful world...
and with deepest appreciation to my friends at
University Christian Church.*

A
Larger
Hope

OPENING
THE HEART
TO GOD

R. SCOTT COLGLAZIER

CHALICE
PRESS
ST. LOUIS, MISSOURI

Biblical quotations, unless otherwise noted, are from the *New Revised Standard Version Bible*, copyright 1989, Division of Christian Education of the National Council of the Churches of Christ in the United States of America. Used by permission. All rights reserved.

The poem "Scraps of Moon" from *This Great Unknowing* by Denise Levertov is reprinted by permission of New Directions Publishing Corp.

The poem "Love After Love" from *Collected Poems 1948–1984* by Derek Walcott is reprinted by permission from Noonday Press.

The untitled poem from *Leaving Home* by Garrison Keillor is reprinted by permission from Penguin Putnam Inc.

The poem "The Swan" from *New and Selected Poems* by Mary Oliver is reprinted by permission of Beacon Press.

Cover art: © Digital Stock
Cover design: Lynne Condellone
Interior design: Elizabeth Wright
Art direction: Michael Domínguez

This book is printed on acid-free, recycled paper.

Visit Chalice Press on the World Wide Web at
www.chalicepress.com

10 9 8 7 6 5 4 3 2 1   02 03 04 05 06 07

Library of Congress Cataloging–in–Publication Data

Colglazier, R. Scott, 1956–
   A larger hope : opening the heart to God / Scott Colglazier.
   p.   cm.
   ISBN 0-8272-2132-0 (alk. paper)
   1. Spiritual life--Christianity. I. Title.
BV4501.3 .C645 2002
248.4' 866–dc21

2002002069

Printed in the United States of America

Table of Contents

Introduction

"Yes, I am a Christian, but I'm not *that* kind of Christian."

More and more, these are the words I find myself thinking, if not actually saying to others, as I try to understand myself, my religious feelings, and my role as a minister and teacher of the Christian faith.

I *am* a Christian. I feel neither shame nor superiority over that profession of faith. I find the story of Jesus engaging. Compelling. Even life-changing. Not only am I interested in the historical dimensions surrounding his life, I'm even more intrigued with what I would call the "spiritual presence" of Jesus, that resonating feeling that the spiritual figure of Jesus lives within my consciousness and is a spiritual companion with me on the journey of faith. My personal search is for a faith that is intellectually coherent and spiritually passionate, a faith that rings true within my everyday experience. My interest in the Christian faith is more than a passing fancy; I have found that connecting my personal story to a larger story of faith is both energizing and meaningful.

Additionally, I'm the senior minister of University Christian Church in Fort Worth, Texas. It is one of the largest and, in the opinion of many, one of the most dynamic Protestant churches in the country. I love the members of this church and often marvel at the depth of their faith. I preach sermons there every Sunday. I do it partly because I have to do it (which means that sometimes I present sermons even when I don't feel like it). On the other hand, I do it because every sermon is a fascinating challenge to make sense of the inner meaning of the Christian faith—not living on the surface, but diving underneath the surface in order to find the essence of my faith experience. It's an exploration that happens not in some academic vacuum, but in the face of aching, heartbreaking human experiences. Each Sunday I share in the sacred symbols of holy communion with the church. Each Sunday I enjoy the company of these people in the congregation. As with my own flawed and very

1

human life, I am at various times impressed with how good they can be, and dismayed with how apathetic and petty they can be. Nevertheless, in the end, we teach one another about what it means to have faith, hanging together like a well-spun spider web, trembling with the events of our lives; but through it all, we continue in the mystery of being a church.

In spite of the fact that I have a well-defined religious vocation, the word *Christian* has become a fragmented word and, in some cases, a wholly unsatisfying one. What *does* it mean to be a Christian? What do Christians *really* believe? How does the Christian faith need to *change* as we begin this new century? What's the true *agenda* of the Christian faith? Is there a way to be Christian while at the same time *participating* deeply in the world? Even more to the point, is there a way of being a Christian without being *embarrassed* by it? To those of you who just attend church from time to time, never really giving much thought to the connection of life and faith, these questions may seem odd, especially coming from a minister. But I have a hunch that many of you reading this book know exactly what I mean when I ask these questions, questions of what it means to have an authentic faith and a larger hope for the future of Christianity.

At a recent General Assembly of the Christian Church (Disciples of Christ), I had two chance encounters with two very different church leaders. My experience of meeting these leaders continues to speak to me in all of its contradiction and cacophony, reminding me that there is little consensus over what it means to be a Christian. I would suggest these two conversations represent two divergent directions that Christians are choosing today, choices that will shape the identity of Christianity in the twenty-first century.

One leader was a well-known conservative gadfly. In his magazine, he is forever arguing for an approach to faith that includes a classical view of God, a literal interpretation of the Bible, a condemnation toward gay and lesbian persons, and an overall stance toward the Christian faith that lacks openness or flexibility. Maybe I'm particularly sensitive toward him because after the publication of my first book, *Finding a Faith That Makes Sense*, he gave it a scathing review. But in retrospect, it wasn't a review at all. It was more a diatribe from someone who approaches faith from a literalistic, legalistic starting place, and though we are both Christians, members of the same denomination, and even though we attend church at our respective congregations week after week, the starting places for our faith are so starkly different that it feels as if we have little or nothing in common. As I walked away from him in that cavernous downtown convention center, I couldn't help but think, *We may be members of the same denomination, but we live in different universes!*

In other words, "I am a Christian, but I'm not *that* kind of Christian."

To be sure, he would say the same thing about me.

The other person I met was a professor I studied with at Christian Theological Seminary in Indianapolis several years ago. He is a person I both admire and respect, and he's also someone who has had a tremendous influence on my own theological development. When I first met him, he was a young professor fresh out of the University of Chicago. In my eyes, he was open and smart and sophisticated. He unlocked my mind to various thinkers like Paul Ricoeur and Paul Tillich, masterfully integrated the Christian faith with his interest in contemporary Jewish literature, and on top of all that, worked passionately for the ecumenical vision of the church. Most of all, he always engaged larger and larger conversations about faith and religion and world. For him, the Christian faith seemed to be a pathway toward the deeper issues of life, not a system of truth to be defined and defended, and not merely a destination at which one arrived, but a true adventure. The Christian faith that radiated from his life was an exciting, open, inspiring process. Seeing him in that convention center was a moment of pure joy, evoking that rare feeling of being at home with another human being. The connection, however, was more than personal; it was as if there were a shared vision between us, as if we were of the same body.

The juxtaposition of these two conversations within a matter of about ten minutes continues to haunt me. But in a way that transcends my personal experience that day, I think the larger issues unwittingly symbolized by these two leaders haunt virtually every Protestant church in America today.

American Protestant churches are undergoing a time-lapse earthquake. And not just a few of them. All of them. All of them are in a theological crisis. All of them are experiencing a growing chasm of faith. All of them have a jagged fault line splitting the bedrock of their congregational lives. Granted, some congregations seem to hold together better than others, and in fact, one sign of a healthy church is being able to hold certain theological tensions together; but that tensions exist is undeniable. My perception is that Christians are having a harder and harder time defining what it means to be a Christian. It goes deeper than the style of worship a church might employ. It goes deeper than mere denominational affiliation, which increasingly means less and less. Under review—and what an exciting review it is—is *the fundamental question of what it means to be a Christian*, and particularly, *the challenge of being nurtured by the fundamentals of the faith without having to be a religious fundamentalist.*

How is it that two people can be in the same church but be so far apart in terms of faith and belief, have such radically different postures toward life itself, and in effect, be people who, for all practical purposes, believe in different religions? Why are American Main Street religious communities—Methodist churches, Baptist churches, Presbyterian churches, Episcopal churches—so fragmented around questions of belief and perspective? Is it the case, as we turn the corner into a new millennium, that two broadly conceived *styles* or *types* or *genres* of Christians are developing—so much so that people think of themselves as *this* kind of Christian but not *that* kind of Christian, at once an affirmation of faith and a disclaimer of faith?

Some Christians, for example, listen to the conservative advice of Dr. James Dobson each day on a local Christian radio station. Some are shaped by fundamental approaches to Bible study, often putting more energy into their Bible study groups than they do in their own congregations. Some attend religious retreats designed to create powerful religious experiences, often insisting that unless people have the same kind of Christian experience, theirs is not valid at all. Some hold a faith that is shaped more by a television evangelist than by their own congregational pastor. Still others believe in a classical God who supposedly answers prayer much like a mail-order catalog operation, or they believe in a literal theory of inspiration that claims the Bible is the unalterable word of God, complete and without error, or they believe in a literal second coming of Jesus, a concept heightened by millennial fever and fueled by a best-selling series of novels called the *Left Behind* series, or they believe the Christian religion is the only religion and therefore support proselytizing efforts toward people of other faiths, or they believe in a literal creation story and believe creationism should be taught in schools. The list could go on and on and on. And it does go on and on.

None of these issues are new to the American religious landscape. What is notable, however, is that some of these people are Presbyterian and some are Episcopalian and some are Methodist and some are Lutheran and some are members of the Christian Church (Disciples of Christ). In other words, traditional, mainline, mainstream, Main Street–type churches are experiencing a widening theological fissure that is as serious as anything American Christians have ever faced. Over the past ten years, significant attention has been given to the decline of membership and financial resources of mainline Protestant churches. However, these issues are like intramural sports compared to the larger theological issues pressing themselves to the forefront of congregational life. What does it mean to be a Christian? What do Christians believe and practice? What is at the heart of the Christian story?

T. S. Eliot once wrote, "We shall not cease from our exploration."[1] It is precisely this spirit of invitation, of journey, that goes to the heart of the Jesus message. I think of that wonderful story of Jesus healing a blind man. When the man begins to see, he sees people walking around looking like tall, elongated trees. We typically think of the Jesus touch as bringing instantaneous healing. How much we want this in life! Instant success. Instant weight loss. Instant intimacy. Instant gratification. And we also want instant religion and faith and answers. Truth be told, we probably want instant God. Yet God is not instant. There are layers to work through, experiences to be understood, conversations to be visited over and over and over again. It takes a certain amount of courage to see the world as inhabited by walking trees. But distortion is often a precursor to clarity.

In this particular encounter with a blind man, found in the gospel of Mark, Jesus engages the man's brokenness not once but twice, and if twice, then we can imagine it could happen again and again. Nothing instantaneous. Nothing that eliminates the ongoing exploration of what it means to see. Could it be that the underlying message is that there are no shortcuts to God? In many ways, the Christian gospel is about seeing, seeing the world differently, ourselves differently, even seeing God differently. This kind of seeing is not found in simplistic answers, nor is it discovered by narrow, rigid, simplistic explanations. Instead, faith calls for an ongoing conversation with the deepest demands and longings of the soul. Emily Dickinson captured it well when, in one of her poems, she suggested that it is not "revelation" we need, but a new perspective for our "unfurnished eyes."[2] The faith journey is an exploration given to us as a gift from God. And maybe, just maybe, the exploration *is* God.

Understanding faith as a journey is not a new metaphor for the spiritual life, but it's the one that is becoming more and more crucial as the American religious landscape shifts with cultural aftershocks. There are "answer" churches out there and then there are "journey" churches; "answer" Christians and "journey" Christians; and of course "answer" ministers and "journey" ministers. I am unashamedly a "journey" Christian, and it's my joy to lead a "journey" congregation and to be a "journey" minister in its midst. Personally, I think the best of American Protestantism has always been characterized by an understanding of faith as journey and a vision of life as pilgrimage, but it's more than Protestantism, and it's even more than Christianity. Journey is what it means to be alive in the most human sense of that word.

My friend Forrest Church defines religion as "our human response to the dual reality of being alive and having to die."[3] Think of it: Between birth and death there exists the great journey of being alive. We may try to fill that time with lockbox answers, but I suspect we try to fill it with answers because we are afraid of the ambiguity of the experience itself. Yet to have faith is not so much about collecting answers as it is discovering the essence of spiritual courage, and it is courage that we need for the journey. Maybe it's the case that Christians should be defined not by *what* we know but by *whom* we know, not by the answers we can give but by the questions we are courageous enough to ask. That's what it means for me to be a Christian, and I know of no other way to live the journey than by opening wide the heart to God. The poet Rainer Maria Rilke has written, "Let no place in me hold itself closed, for where I am closed, I am false."[4] I think that's what faith in God is about, opening the heart as wide as possible between the two great mysteries of birth and death, finding the truth of God and the truth of ourselves.

I think it's fair to say that most people don't have a theology, at least not in the technical sense of the word *theology*. However, what people do have are spiritual feelings or thoughts or experiences. In other words, few people are theologians, but everyone is religious. I'm sure if I could sit down and talk personally to everyone reading this book, you might tell me about your spiritual experiences or you would talk about those two or three core ideas that shape your religious consciousness. Your spirituality might be shaped by the experience when your first child was born. Or the time your mother passed away. Or the time you walked on the beach and the sunset was so stunningly beautiful that the beauty moved you to tears. Or the time you forgave someone. Or the time you prayed for God's forgiveness and felt a sense of peace wash over you like a wave of love. These are the spiritual experiences we need to listen to, learn from, share with one another. Ultimately, the center of faith has to incorporate these genuine experiences of life.

I'm more and more convinced that this is exactly what Jesus did. He left behind no systematic commentary on the Torah. No organized theology. No systematic philosophy of life. He didn't write a book. Furthermore, Jesus never preached a biblical sermon. Instead, Jesus said things like, "Consider the lilies of the field..." Or "Notice the mustard seed, notice how tiny it really is..." Or "There once was a father who had two sons..." Or "There was a man traveling from Jerusalem to

Jericho…" Jesus listened to life, life in general but also his own life, and then he told stories and parables and tossed out God-images like a pitcher throwing batting practice before the seventh game of the World Series. Interestingly enough, one of the criticisms leveled against Jesus was that he wasn't religious enough. Ah, but he was religious, just not in a systematic, linear way, not in a give-all-the-answers kind of way. The reason there should be "journey" churches and "journey" ministers and "journey" Christians is because Jesus of Nazareth lived a "journey" life. His theology emerged from his experiences in life, experiences that became like little clusters of spiritual nerves, and it is around these clusters that his theology eventually touched the world.

My hope is that this book is also a "journey" book. I wrote it for all those friends I have met, some inside the church, some not, but men and women searching for a Christian faith that resonates within the deepest places of the heart. Maybe you go to church. Maybe you don't. Maybe you go to a church, but you find yourself hard-pressed to believe in a literal, narrow, fundamental kind of faith. Perhaps you are looking for some theological fresh air, some room and space and permission to be theologically and emotionally free before God. Maybe you want to explore your faith a little deeper. In short, this book is written for any who are ready to open their hearts to a larger hope, a larger faith in a good and gracious and life-inspiring God.

CHAPTER ONE

Honoring the Religious Heart

*Like Buddha, Jesus directed people to the sacred kingdom
within. Both taught that enlightenment came through the
development of an imaginative vision that can transform
each of us as individuals and help bring about the
enlightenment of others. Jesus also continued the tradition of
his own forebears, the Hebrew prophets and psalmists, who
held incessant dialogues with the world of the spirit and
preached that our supreme good lies in maintaining rightful
relationships to its unseen order. How did one go about
this? Through the heart, the seat of wisdom and
understanding.*

GAIL GODWIN[1]

Not long ago I was on a flight from New York City to Dallas–
Fort Worth, and I happened to be seated next to a young woman
who was in her late twenties. To be honest, I rarely strike up
conversations with people on airplanes. It's a great time to read
and write, plus, I figure there's little chance of building much
of a relationship during a three-hour flight. However, for reasons

I still don't quite understand, this young woman was different. Something about her honesty, her genuineness, something about the intensity of her search, has stayed with me.

She was holding in her hand a book on Buddhism. I asked her about it, and she told me she was in the process of a spiritual exploration. A personal kind of search. We talked about Buddhism a little bit. I told her that I too, in spite of the fact that I'm a Christian minister, find Buddhist teachings quite insightful and had studied at a Buddhist retreat center. I also learned over the course of the flight that she was a social worker in New York. That she didn't make much money but she loved her job and loved living on the Upper West Side of Manhattan. That her parents were divorced. That she had developed some pretty damaging personal habits when she was a teenager, but through some counselors at school and support from a few mentors, she had moved past all of that. She liked working with young people because she could relate to some of their struggles. She also said that she didn't have much of a religious background. That her mother would take her to the Episcopal church every now and then when she was a kid, but she basically grew up in California with very little religious grounding.

What I remember most about the conversation, what was and is still seared upon my mind, are these words. She said, *"I'm so desperate to really believe in something."*

My gut-level response, even though I didn't share it with her that day, my unedited, visceral, silent response was, *"So am I, my friend, so am I."*

I long to believe in something. Something. Not anything, but something. That something I want to believe in is real and ultimate, it is resonant with truth and beauty and authenticity. That something is near and far, within and beyond. To believe, or to want to believe, is just another way of saying that I want to be connected to my life. Connected to the world in which I live. But to find that connection means I have to be willing to honor the journey my heart wants to take. And I choose to talk about it in that way. The heart wants to take a journey. It's not that I merely decide at an ego level to follow a spiritual journey or undertake a religious search. The ego has a role to play, but I'm more and more convinced that the heart chooses it for us. Or as Emily Dickinson once wrote to a friend, "The heart wants what it wants." The heart is like a racehorse in the gate, ready to be released, ready to run, ready to follow the path toward God. Therefore, what we have to be willing to do is ride the great horse-heart where it wants to go.

As a child, I remember going to church on Sunday mornings, seeing the candles burning in the sanctuary, the choir processing in their colorful robes, listening to the sounds of the pipe organ, at times so loud that it would literally vibrate the floor of the church and shake the pews in which I would sit and squirm. I had no concept as a little boy that one way of even thinking about God, the divine energy of the universe, is that God is the true vibrato of the world, and that to touch and be touched by the divine vibrato was in fact the purpose of my humanity. The whole Sunday morning picture created a fascination for me, even a heightened awareness that there is more to life, more to my young human experience than what I could see or hear. It was as if the whole world was teeming with life right underneath the skin of my observations, and though I did not understand it, I loved it. Moreover, I wanted more of it. I wanted to explore it and touch it, and most of all, I wanted to be connected to it. In some ways, I think it's fair to say that my spiritual journey started with a lit candle in a church sanctuary.

My sense, and I know there are those who would argue the point, is that this capacity for a connection with the universe is one of the hallmark characteristics of what it means to be a human being. It is our religious capacity, our potential for meaning and exploration, alas, it is our spiritual emptiness, that is only filled by the divine presence. The great energy we need for our living is neither oil nor gas nor coal, nor is it nuclear or solar or wind. The great energy we need is God. Consequently, I believe that within every human being there broods an energy source, the deepest reservoir of activity within the human psyche—it is the energy of God—and this energy constitutes who you are and who you can become. Therefore, one way to talk about the spiritual life is to talk about the possibility of connecting to that energy.

It doesn't really matter to me how the energy is named. You can call it G-O-D. God. You might want to call it the divine spirit or divine energy. You can call it Christ. The spirit of Christ.

The energy of Christ. You can call it creative, loving, transforming energy. You can call it the indwelling of the Holy Spirit. The Spirit of truth. The Spirit of love. The Spirit of hope. You can call it the Spirit that strengthens our inner spirit. (An expression from the apostle Paul, and one which I like very much.) You can call it the spirit of life or just call it creativity; it doesn't really matter. You might want to take the lead of Jesus and call it "The kingdom of God within you." (I love that expression.) The kingdom of God is neither here nor there, and it's not out there anymore than it's over there. The kingdom of God is within you. You could call it the life force. Call it the holy, the other, the transcendent force of the universe that is above all and in all and through all. Fine. I don't even mind if you call it Eros, that mythic energy linking heaven and earth, the energy that opens up ecstasy and awe and wonder. Sometimes I think another word for it is simply heart.

Call it whatever you want to call it, because I'm not worried about the language. After all, any language we use, including Christian language, biblical language, the language of all world religions—when it's all added up it still falls short in naming that which is unnameable. Surely we know that the word *God* is not the same as God. The word *Christ* is not the same as Christ. The word *Spirit* is not the Spirit.

What I'm talking about is an energy that moves inside the deepest places of our human experience; therefore, the language we use is not nearly as important as the recognition with which we need to experience it; it's this recognition in life that is everything. It is everything. Therefore, I wonder what would it mean for you to connect to that energy, to really honor the heart's capacity to be filled with the transcendent energy of the divine? Is there a way for us to have more energy, more vitality in life? And is there a way to live with a deeper sense of spiritual awareness? To answer these questions means we have to begin a religious search. Even those of us who are in church week after week, even those of us leading and directing churches week after week—we need to take up the religious search. To follow the religious heart, its inklings and fascinations, its dreams and impulses, is to be on the trail of God.

There's a parable from the gospel of Matthew I find fascinating, and strangely enough, it's partly because I'm repulsed by it. It's the story of ten bridesmaids waiting to meet a bridegroom. They all have lamps, and they all have oil in their lamps, but only five of them have thought to bring extra oil. In the parable, some are considered wise and some foolish. What happens to five of them, the foolish five, is that they run out of energy. The implication in the parable is that because the groom is delayed, and they run out of oil for their lamps, they miss his appearance, and thus the wedding and celebration. Sadly, the ones who run out of energy are left out in the cold and dark. It doesn't take the keenest of minds to make the quick interpretation that some seem to find God and others don't. Some are in and some are out. Some are good and some are bad. However, rather than using this parable as a commentary on the eternal fate of individuals—something I don't feel qualified to address—I'm drawn to this metaphor of running out of energy. Clearly, we have an energy problem when it comes to oil and gas. As a society we have become dependent on these products, products that we all use, products that damage the environment, products that will eventually be depleted. But there are other kinds of energy crises, crises of human energy.

Look across the landscape of our culture, and what you see is people who are tired. We are tired and fatigued. Worn out and burned out. Many of us are tired and have no idea why we are tired, and so physicians simply name it chronic fatigue syndrome. But even if it is not diagnosed, our culture is suffering from a chronic energy shortage, energy of the spiritual kind. Is our physical fatigue a result of our neglect of the spiritual journey we are called to undertake? Are we tired because we have failed miserably at honoring the needs of the heart? How many people did you run into this week who were having a great day? How many faces in the crowd at the mall or walking downtown during the noon hour radiated any sense of joy and happiness? How many people responded to your "How are you?" this week, by saying, "Superb! Fantastic! Oh, I'm very alive today!" How many people do you know who are alive with anything that resembles a deep kind of spiritual energy?

There is a distinction worth making at this point about styles or paradigms of religious journeys. Some see the journey of faith as this movement toward that which is right, getting right with God, finding the right religion, worshiping the right God in the right way, living the right Christian lifestyle, believing the right beliefs, figuring out the right theology, achieving the right interpretation of the Bible. Interestingly enough, just a few days ago someone handed me a copy of a book that contained a litmus test for finding a "Biblical Church" to attend. Nothing but a religion of being right.

I think this way of conceiving the spiritual journey is misguided for a couple of reasons. To call any church a biblical church or the right church or a correct church is a matter of judgment, a judgment not easily nor accurately made. The same could even be said of other religions, a topic I address later in the book. Not to be overlooked is that Jesus, though completely indebted to his religious tradition, was trying to awaken something in people far deeper than organizational attachment. Jesus understood, as have all great religious leaders, that you can believe all the right things and still miss God. You can belong to a so-called biblical church, or any fundamental religion for that matter, but still never open the heart to the mystery and wonder of faith. The spiritual journey we are called to live is from the heart and toward the heart, which means that when the heart is the ultimate destination, the journey is never completed; it is always an adventure, and it is full of mystery and fear and joy and wonder. It's the true energy of faith.

This is one reason why I have been so interested in spiritual autobiography. In recent years I've read the wonderful volumes of Thomas Merton's journals. Almost every page contains this human search for God. At times Merton is bombastic and confident, at other times, anxious and worrisome. Still at other moments, he is quiet and doubtful and vulnerable. Merton was one of the great spiritual giants of the twentieth century, yet his whole life of faith was a movement toward his own heart and the heart of God. The same could be said for some of the journals of Henri Nouwen. This man lived a very human journey, complete with fear, anxiety, and failure. Starting with Augustine's *Confessions* all the way down to contemporary pilgrims like Anne Lamott or Frederick Buechner, the true essence of the Christian faith has been expressed within the vicissitudes of journey and not arrival. There is a great difference in seeing faith as a subjective autobiographical experience as opposed to an objective research project we're trying to get right.

Even that old standby philosopher Charlie Brown has a good word to say about the spiritual journey. Charlie Brown was lying in bed late one night and said to himself, "Sometimes I lie awake at night, and I ask, 'Is life a multiple choice test or is it a true or false test?'" The next frame he says, "Then a voice comes to me out of the dark and says, 'We hate to tell you this, but life is a thousand-word essay.'" My sense is that many have taken the mysteries of faith–the true essay–and turned it into answers and steps and principles. Such a presentation may satisfy our anxious need to have everything in black and white, but it does little to really open up the heart.

There's a wonderful essay by James Carse in which he describes an experience as a boy and the coming to terms with the true nature of the heart's journey. He remembers growing up in Milwaukee, near Lake Michigan, seeing and experiencing the lake in all its many moods and temperatures. But one particular November he was there with his dad, and though the lake itself was quiet, all the vacationers having gone home for the summer, he observed what seemed to his boyish eyes as a million ducks and geese flying over the lake. He opened up one of those rare, unforgettable conversations with his father.

"Where are they going?" he asked his dad.

"South."

"Where's that?"

"Far, very far from here."

"How do they know how to find it?"

"They just know."

"Why don't they stop here?"

"They know this isn't the south."

"Do they know this is Milwaukee?"

"Well, no, they don't know that."

"Are they lost?"

"No."

Carse continues, "This last answer always brought a pause to the conversation. The birds didn't know where they were, but they weren't lost. They knew where they were going, even if they had never been there before. If as adults we are annoyed by questions like this, it is not because they are unanswerable, but because the answers raise even larger questions about the certainties that come with being adults. We know where we are, but are we really so sure we are not lost?…The mind does not come to life until it meets what it cannot comprehend…The wild geese do not know where they are, but they are not lost. Knowledge can lift the veil. It can also become the veil."[2]

"I'm so desperate to really believe in something." There is something so utterly wonderful about that expression, particularly if what is beating inside each word is the willingness to open the heart to the journey. Many of us have either run out of energy for the journey, or we have become so disconnected from it that it feels only like a faint memory, or worse, a cliché. But the heart wants what it wants. Even if all that is left inside our deepest being are ruins, stones and columns piled upon one another, even the ruins whisper an invitation to take up the religious journey.

Therefore, one way to think about faith is finding the courage to be lost. Or to follow Carse, to not know where we are and *not* be lost. To want to believe in something is not the same as getting all the right answers, or having the right information, or fixing our anxious lives with quick solutions. The religious journey, if it is a true journey of the heart, is messy and beautiful, terrifying and comforting, depressing and exhilarating. Yet when it is undertaken, we experience the most important gift imaginable: we become alive. Being alive is what it's all about.

In one of his most inspired moments, the apostle Paul wrote, "A new creation is everything." But to find the new creation requires that we open up the dizzying chaos that whirls within our being, true thoughts and true feelings and true doubts, and then we allow the Spirit of God to sweep across our primordial waters the way it brought order to the universe in the beginning. There was no creation without the mess of mud and muck and water. Likewise, there is no new creation without undertaking the heart's journey. Why some Christians miss this, I really have no explanation for, but the best example for this kind of journey is found in Jesus himself. What draws me to his life is not his triumphs but his vulnerabilities. His willingness to be alone. To sweat tears. To shed blood. To experience his own brokenness while reaching out to touch others. Even his heroic moment in the sun—riding into Jerusalem with the shouts of adoration from the crowds—quickly turned confusing and chaotic. In the hours that followed his parade, there was betrayal, suffering, and death. A case can be made that he did not know where he was, but neither was he lost.

Somewhere between the new creation being everything, and the desire to believe in something, is the heart's true journey. The religious journey. The essence and energy of what it means to be a human being. In the words of the great poet Kabir, "The bee of the heart dives into it and wants no other joy."[3]

CHAPTER TWO

It's All about Listening

I must listen to my life and try to understand what it is truly about—quite apart from what I would like it to be about—or my life will never represent anything real in the world, no matter how earnest my intentions...I must listen to my life telling me who I am. I must listen for the truths and values at the heart of my own identity, not the standards by which I must live—but the standards by which I cannot help but live if I am living my own life.

PARKER PALMER[1]

"How do I begin?" That's exactly the question a friend brought up to me in my office as she sat at a table and looked out the window. The sun was shining. Leaves were beginning to show the greening of spring. Students were walking toward morning classes. "How do I begin?"

She was brought up in the church, has fond memories of Sunday school and youth groups and church camp, but now she was asking different questions of life. She wanted to know how to start living a life of faith. She wanted to know how to nurture her faith, her spiritual feelings, in a way that was real and vital and meaningful; connected to the church, but not overwhelmed by the church either. She wasn't so much looking for answers as she was looking for a centered way of thinking about her spiritual life and the church, a faith that could become a single tapestry of sensibility and vitality.

It's interesting to me how many people have strong beliefs, but their beliefs are never woven into the fabric of their spiritual experiences. It's as if their beliefs are isolated islands floating in a different universe. And beliefs that don't resonate with life, in the end, aren't really beliefs at all. On the other hand, many people I know have spiritual feelings, but they never seem to connect the dots of their feelings to the stories and teachings of the Christian gospel. Our individual stories are essential, but if we never connect them to a larger story, they begin to look like raisins, withered and dried. Surely, there has to be a way to create a patchwork quilt of wholeness within the Christian experience–thoughts, feelings, beliefs, and behaviors all stitched together into a coherent life.

One of the hallmark characteristics of a faith is listening. Listening is no mere add-on to a long list of Christian duties, nor can it be reduced to one of several spiritual steps we take toward God. Real listening, the kind of listening we do within our souls, to our souls, to the stories of others, to the experiences we have in the common world of everyday life, even the listening we attempt with ancient scripture stories that are an inexhaustible source of inspiration, is crucial to the life of faith. Too many times we think of religion as something we get "over there." We go to some external source or authority. But the best expression of religion is always an experience of deep listening.

One of the great joys of being in a family is the talking and listening that goes on over the course of a lifetime. Sometimes it's around the dinner table. Maybe early in the morning as people are leaving for school or work. In our house, Sunday night has become our time of listening. We almost always cook together. Eat together. Preferably outside on the patio. (A patio my son and I built, by the way.) We never know what the conversation will be about; maybe it will be about a book or movie, maybe about what is coming up this week or next, maybe about how church went earlier in the day. (It's one of the hazards of a minister's family.) But a real household is characterized by listening.

The same is true of a real faith experience. Listening implies dialogue. Listening implies surprise and wonder and imagination. Listening implies a living relationship. Listening implies complexity and layers and the peeling back of human fear and hope. I'm always amazed that Christians of a more fundamental persuasion place their emphasis upon a faith that must be adhered to and followed in some kind of slavish, literal way, believing somehow that God has lowered a system of faith down from the sky like a prop from the ceiling of a theater, and our job is to follow every comma and period of the system. Oftentimes the emphasis is on obeying God. My concern about this approach is that it reinforces fear, eliminates freedom, douses creativity. Not to be overlooked, the word *obedience* actually means to listen, to really listen to the deepest voices of God. Obedience as listening is so much more than an observance of rules. When faith is a conversation, we are not only allowed but are encouraged to pay attention to our feelings and experiences, to engage in a process of faith that is exploration and that, it seems to me, is the beginning of the spiritual life.

Maybe a brief reflection on what I think is one of the most fascinating encounters ever recorded between Jesus and another human being will be helpful on this topic of listening. It's the story of Jesus and the Samaritan woman, found in the gospel of John, a vivid portrayal of a woman who desperately needed to listen to her own life.

Jesus was sitting by a well in the middle of town. It could have been a Starbucks. It could have been a coffee shop on the Left Bank in Paris (Café de Flore, of course). Could have been a Barnes & Noble bookstore. Doesn't really matter. He was just sitting there, sitting there and waiting, available and waiting for conversation. Don't overlook, however, the symbolism of the well. The well represents depth in life, refreshment and meaning in life. And it's available. Waiting and available for anyone, for me, for you, for that Samaritan woman.

She comes to the well at noon looking for water, and Jesus strikes up a fascinating conversation with her. He asks her for a drink of water. This may look like a conversation about water, but it's not merely about water. It's about finding joy and meaning and hope in life. It's about finding divine depth in life. It's about discovering the real source of life in life. That's what water means in this particular story.

What Jesus attempts to do in this encounter is to help the woman listen to the depth of her own experience. That's where religion begins. Spirituality begins the very moment we find the courage to listen to our lives. Not surprisingly, I am more and more convinced that that's what Jesus was all about. Jesus doesn't arrive on the scene selling some product like a tacky infomercial. He doesn't say, "Boy, do I really have something over here you need." No, that wasn't his message. Religion doesn't begin with a book. Nor with a creed. Nor with a doctrine. Instead, Jesus seems to say to people again and again, "There is really something inside *you* that you need, that you need to pay attention to, that you need to listen to, that you need to set free into the world; and until you do, until you really begin to listen to what is already inside your soul, you will never find God."

This kind of approach to faith is one reason why people found Jesus so compelling. This is why I continue to find Jesus so compelling. He wasn't asking people to become something they weren't; he was asking people to become who they really were and are, people who could love and be loved, people who could be compassionate and receive compassion, people who could be good and do good in the world, people who have inside them a God-spring just waiting to bubble up and gurgle and flow upward into everyday life.

Jesus encounters this Samaritan woman, and what happens is that in a variety of ways she deflects the very opportunity Jesus is giving her to listen to her life. For example, the first thing she says to him is: "Why in the world would a Jewish man take time to speak to me, a Samaritan woman?"

What the woman doesn't understand is that Jesus loves the soul of the woman. He loves her humanity and potential as a human being. That's why he knocks down gender barriers like a bulldozer. He's after the inside of people. That's why he knocks down the walls of prejudice dividing Samaritans and Jews like a demolition crane. He's after the inside of men and women. Because what he knows is that if people can begin to touch God on the inside, then all that stuff on the outside, particularly all the religious stuff on the outside, isn't really that important. Or better said, it's important in all the right ways.

But the woman deflects him again. This time she brings up the fact that this well in the middle of town is really the well where God blessed Jacob. Oh yes, Jacob's well. But I wonder, is she really interested in this historical landmark, or is she doing what so many of us do, namely, bringing up the past in order to deflect the present spiritual opportunity we have with God? That is, sometimes we live in the past so we don't have to move into the future. Sometimes we use the past as a mask to hide behind so we don't have to face what really needs to be faced in our lives today. Jesus seemed to know this about the woman; therefore, instead of taking the bait of history, he tries to move her to listen to her life again. He says, "I'm not interested in Jacob's well. I'm interested in the well that is inside of you, that place where the Spirit of God lives inside of you, the very Spirit that can gush forth like an Evian geyser inside of you; that's what I'm interested in, not some excursion into the past, but an embrace of the spiritual present."

Let me tell you about a thrilling moment I had during the summer of 2000. I had a chance to go to France during the month of July. It was my first time to take a trip like this, and I loved it. It was wonderful beyond words, but one of the most thrilling moments I had on the trip was being in Paris on the very last day of the Tour de France bicycle race. I found a place on the side of the street where I knew the cyclists would be coming through and planted myself behind a police barricade. I really wanted to see this. This race is one of the great athletic challenges of modern times, and so I waited to see it. You can guess who I really wanted to see; I wanted to see Lance Armstrong, *the* Lance Armstrong from Austin, Texas.

The police motorcycles went by, and then the sponsor cars went by, and then the team cars went by, and then I saw them, all those cyclists coming around the corner wearing their bright uniforms, speeding down a long stretch of Paris street, fans cheering wildly. They love their cycling in Europe! And then he went right past me wearing his yellow jersey. Lance Armstrong, 1999 winner, 2000 winner. I was probably ten feet away from him as he whizzed by on his bicycle, and I wanted to say something, I wanted to yell something, and all I could think to scream in the middle of Paris was: "I'm from Texas!" I'm not sure, but I think he looked at me. I do know that little Frenchman standing next to me gave me a look like I was from a different planet, but I think Lance Armstrong saw me that day.

Later when he was crowned the winner of the Tour de France, I saw him with his wife, his child, saw him hold up the winner's check. But what I really saw was a human story behind that amazing athletic achievement. Here was a man who only a few years earlier had had cancer. Here was a man who had every reason to let the past ruin his future, who could have used the past as an excuse to miss the present. But he didn't. And the fact that he didn't is more remarkable than winning the Tour de France. And I would also add, it is completely consistent with the presence of Jesus; although Jesus understands our past just as we must learn to listen to our past, Jesus wants us to be more than that.

Jesus tries to move this Samaritan woman past gender barriers, past cultural barriers, even past historical barriers, but she still doesn't quite get the point. The living water of Jesus is not in some well; it's really inside her, and he's offering it to her, but she's still not paying attention to it, at least not at the depth of which she is capable. So Jesus tries another tack. He says, "Why don't you go back home and get your husband and come back to see me." Ah, the moment of truth has arrived. She says, "Well, you see Jesus, I, well, I, you see, well, I don't really have a husband." He says, "You're right. You have had five husbands. And the one you're with right now isn't really your husband."

Ooohhh…that would be called the *direct approach* to conversation. But do you see what he's trying to get her to do? He wants her to listen to her life. One way to think about it is this: In our most intimate, most significant relationships we sustain some degree of brokenness. It happens in every single marriage. It happens in every family. It happens in our professions. But to have had not just one but two, but three, but four, but five ex-spouses, can you imagine the personal, emotional, psychological, spiritual, financial brokenness this woman had to have been carrying around in her life? Talk about baggage! It's the baggage of the human experience. What Jesus knew about her, and what he knows about us, is that we can't really find a faith until we are courageous enough to begin listening to some of the brokenness that is within us. I think it's important to see that Jesus wasn't trying to embarrass or shame the woman. (Too often religion heaps guilt and shame upon the human spirit.) Jesus was, I think, trying to get her to be honest with her life. Because it's only when we are honest with our thoughts, our feelings, our hurts, our dreams, that we begin to find God. .

This is why I told that woman who was asking such a simple question in my office that day, "Why don't you take the next couple of months and pay attention to your life. Pay attention to your memories. Pay attention to your aspirations. Are they really you? Pay attention to your feelings. Pay attention to your attitudes. Are you really happy being angry all the time? Do you ever get tired of trying to control everyone all the time? Do you ever get exhausted being bitter all the time? What about God? What kind of feelings do you have about God? What do you really believe about God? Do you ever feel that wonderful feeling of being loved by God? If not, why? Just listen. Write your thoughts in a journal. Pray, but let your praying be more listening than talking. Just listen. Just listen."

It's only when we are willing to listen to our lives that we can become real, and it's only when we are willing to be real that we can find God. I remember Brother David Steindl-Rast talking in a workshop many years ago about *The Velveteen Rabbit.* One of the toy animals had this aching desire to become real. And so, one night while all the children were sleeping, a teddy bear asked the wise old rocking horse, "Does it hurt to become real?" And the answer was: "When you become real, you no longer mind the hurt."[2]

I used to think that Jesus was trying to transform me *from* myself. (Faith that is too focused on a conversion metaphor

tends to emphasize this aspect of experience.) There is a place
for conversion, I don't want to deny that, but more and more I
think the issue is how Jesus can help transform me *into* myself.
I now believe that every day I wake up, Jesus is saying
something like, "All right! Let's see if I can transform this man
into the person he is capable of becoming, help him realize his
beauty and goodness. Let's see if the miracle of a new creation
can happen today." Becoming real, listening for what is real,
that is the pathway to God.

That's what was happening with Jesus and this Samaritan
woman. Yet she deflected him one more time. It didn't have to
be that way. She could have been honest and said something
like, "Five husbands. Five broken relationships. Jesus, do you
have any idea how utterly hurt and broken and ashamed I feel
about my life? Do you think there's any hope for me, Jesus?
Do you think there is any way I can start again, Jesus?" She
could have listened to her life and said something like that. But
she didn't.

Instead, she brings up an old theological issue. "You see,
Jesus, Samaritans believe that Mount Gerizim is a holy place,
but you believe that Mount Sinai is a holy place, and we
worship God one way, but you worship God another way,
dadadadadadadadadada !" Do you see what she is doing now?
She's using religion like a ping-pong paddle to knock God to
the other side of the net. Nothing like using religion to deflect
God! She uses the tradition of her worship as a barrier between
herself and the very Spirit that should be inspiring worship in
the first place.

Maybe Jesus grew impatient with her, I don't know, but he
finally summarized the entire encounter by saying, "The essence
of God is spirit; therefore, the only way to really connect with
God is in the depths of your spirit, which is your deepest passion
and feeling for life, and the only way to really know God is to
know your self, being truthful, authentic, real with everything
inside your own soul that resonates with God, and the only
way that is going to happen is if you are willing to listen. That's
the water I'm offering you to drink."

I think it's the water Jesus is still offering people to drink.
It's the privilege, the opportunity, the adventure of listening to

our lives. Spirituality is not something we add on to life, and religion is not like building an addition on to your house. True faith is the essence of our existence. It's the beginning point. The end point. It's every point in between. It's what it means to be alive. A true ecu-faith is more focused on what is happening on the inside of the soul rather than getting all the correct information on the outside of the church. Opening the heart is always about listening.

CHAPTER THREE

The Weight of Perfection

God has given you a beautiful self. There God dwells and loves you with the first love, which precedes all human love. You carry your own beautiful self in your heart.

HENRI NOUWEN[1]

The Christian faith has not always been kind to the soul. Guilt. Repression. Heavy-handed moralism. It's almost a standing joke that religion and guilt go hand in hand. Why is it so hard for many of us to feel what Henri Nouwen called this "beautiful self" in our daily experience of living? Instead of feeling beautiful, Christians often feel unworthy or unacceptable, often feeling more like spiritual failures than beautiful stars shining upon a night canvas. We come to church and feel undeserving. We run a low-grade fever of spiritual insufficiency. Frequently, God is lifted up as the perfect standard, and of course, everything falls short of a perfect God, everything including ourselves. Therefore, instead of faith's being a celebration of the heart, it becomes the heavy baggage of the soul.

27

I remember hearing Rabbi Harold Kushner tell an audience at University Christian Church a few years ago, "When religion is done right, it is very beautiful and life-giving; when it is not done right, it is damaging and deadly to the soul." When I think of a larger hope for the church, I'm thinking about how faith can truly liberate human experience, pulsing with love, with joy, creating larger and larger capacities for passionate living.

Several years ago I knew a woman by the name of Suzanne. She was a member of my church. She always sat on the back pew. Her arms crossed. Legs crossed. Lips pursed tightly, revealing a minuscule circle of wrinkles around her mouth. She looked like she had just stepped out of a Talbot's catalog sitting there with her husband, her teenage son, her daughter. They looked like the perfect family. From the pulpit of that awe-inspiring church I looked at her Sunday after Sunday, and my impression was always that she seemed to look closed off, shut down, somehow weighted down by an invisible force of perfection.

She smiled a lot, but I suspected there was something artificial about it, like she was wearing a mask rather than a genuine face. My reaction toward her was not one of dislike, but a strange mixture of curiosity and compassion and not a little self-reflection about my own spiritual life. I know what it's like to smile and preach and pray Sunday after Sunday even though my soul is somewhere else, even though my soul is weighted down by some invisible burden, including the burden of not being good enough for myself or the church. I couldn't help but wonder what was on the inside of Suzanne's soul. Where was the joy, the ease, the graceful sense of life-flow that women and men can experience? And in terms of the faith experience, I wondered: Does faith finally enliven or deaden the human experience? Does worship ultimately inspire living? Does participation in a community of faith make us more alive, or does it finally drain what little life-energy we have left at the end of the day? If indeed Suzanne was weighted down by some sort of religious perfectionism, then what love or compassion or word might serve to liberate her, or in the words of the rock singer Sting, what might "Free, free, set her free"?

Suzanne was in church every Sunday. My guess is that she was there out of some sense of religious duty, obedience in the worst sense of the word. There out of a large, almost cosmic obligation toward God, there out of some moral compulsion that she was supposed to be there. And my guess is that she was there primarily because she was afraid of *not* being there, afraid that if she wasn't there or if she didn't have her family there that God might punish her or be displeased with her. Being in church on Sunday morning was just part of the system, a religious system she had narrowly defined for herself. Seeing her week after week, I wondered if religion had become part of a larger system of perfectionism. (It comes in so many different forms.) Making her children dress in a certain way was part of the system. Being respectable in the community was part of the system. Never veering from a set of rules, implementing certain behaviors, turning the Bible into a literal answer book were parts of the system. However defined and whatever the source, it all adds up to the heavy weight of perfection.

Implicit in her system of perfection was the confidence that if she kept her end of the bargain, God would be pleased with her, life would turn out more or less well for her and her family, and after a lifetime of doing right things, God would reward her with a place to live throughout all eternity, that place sometimes called heaven. This was her system, or at least so it seemed, and she sat with it Sunday after Sunday on the back pew of the church. For Suzanne, life had become deadly serious. And so had her faith. Heavy. Industrial. Dutiful.

Do you know what it's like to have your heart closed? To have experiences or attitudes or feelings that shut down love or hope or joy inside your life? If so, then you know something of the glorious and painful struggle of becoming an alive human being. I suspect that in Suzanne's case, God was understood as the giver of rules, the master architect of the cosmic blueprint for life. To keep the rules is to please God. To break the rules is to displease God.

What's interesting to me is that Jesus himself was a kind of rule-breaker and, in fact, told stories and parables in order for people to see that there was a different way of thinking about

God and, since faith is always existential, a different way of thinking about ourselves. In the gospel of Matthew, for example, he tells the story of a man who has a vineyard. Early in the morning he hires people to work for a certain hourly wage. What's fascinating in this story is that the people first hired early in the morning negotiate their compensation. So much work, so much pay. Everything is cut and dried. Yet as the day goes on, the owner hires more people. And then more people. Finally, near the end of the day the owner hires some workers for the last hour of the day. Yes, they only work *one* hour. When the closing bell sounds and the workday is completed, the owner begins doling out the checks. The first group, who have worked all day, receive exactly what they bargained for. They are treated fairly by the owner. However, they continue to mill around, watching the owner pay all the other workers. By the time he hands out checks to those who have barely broken a sweat with only one hour of work, they notice these workers receive exactly what they have just been paid–a full day's wage. At first they are incredulous. And then angry. And then they cry out, "Unfair!" and "Unjust!"

Jesus, however, is driving home a point with this upside-down story. Although God is just, God is also gracious and compassionate. God wants to treat people, not merely justly and fairly, but graciously, generously, extravagantly. The essence of God is overflowing love. Abundance and fullness characterize the divine essence. Certainly one can choose to relate to God in a tit-for-tat way. Negotiating the obligation and then trying to fulfill it. One can choose to live a life of measuring up to God, but how dreary! How deadening! How utterly devoid of joy and celebration!

One word for God's creative, transforming love is grace, and grace is God's treating people not according to how they *should* be treated, but in the way God desires to treat them, and the deepest desire of God, at least according to Jesus, is the desire of love. Love always comes to us as a surprise. It may not be surprising, but it feels like a surprise, and we feel wonder and awe in the face of it. Ultimately, love is what opens the heart.

It would be hard to estimate the number of Christians who were given a rigid, oppressive, demanding kind of faith from their parents and churches and Sunday school classes. Hard to estimate the number of churches that continue to propagate this kind of oppressive approach to faith. And sadly, it would be hard to comprehend the amount of damage such a religious framework can do to a person's soul. Where do I stand with God? Is it the case that God loves me because I've done right things? And what about those times when I don't do the right things? Does God love me then? Does God love me when I do something wrong? When I think wrong thoughts? When I have wrong attitudes? Is God over against my humanity, or deeply within it like a friend, a companion, a lover?

Religious perfectionism, at least for the person who has some degree of sensitivity and honesty, becomes a grinding cycle of guilt and, on occasion, even despair. Guilt over not being good enough. Guilt over not having done enough. Guilt over not having felt enough. Here we are walking upon the curvature of this beautiful planet and living within this dazzling universe. We are breathing oxygen and dancing on a cosmic sunbeam every second of our lives. We are capable of feeling love and joy and peace, we can fall in love with a man or woman, hold the miracle of a child in our arms, be enraptured by mountains and oceans and sunsets, but we take faith in God and turn it into a deadening experience. It's no wonder the heart shuts down with that kind of religious orientation. Surely the experience of faith is about something other than fear and guilt.

And if the heart doesn't close down under the weight of religious perfectionism, then the heart closes down with a kind of pernicious self-righteousness. Either I'm no good at all, or, on the arrogant side of the equation, I feel as if I'm better than everyone else. But when we live within a boxed-up world of self-righteousness, we miss the tantalizing joy of daily life and particularly the joy of sharing life with others. How wearisome it is to always have to be better than everyone else. The heart closes off from other people through harsh judgment and aloofness and isolation. Other people are never quite good enough. Other people are always to blame. After all, how can I really open my heart to another human being when I'm attempting to create a nailed-down, glued-down, boarded-up religious world inside my soul, a world in which I'm either protected from or superior to the existence of others? This kind of faith creates a frighteningly lonely world, a world in which we neither give nor receive love.

What I continue to discover within myself is that the world, and God, who is at the heart of the world, is radically gracious. There is no so-called "plan of salvation" to follow. (Although some try to reduce the mysterious complexity of religion to a mere plan.) There is no ultimate judgment day when all deeds will be reviewed. (Judgment day is every day. Every day is a day of existential decision.) Jesus knew this when he invited people to follow him. When is the time right? For Jesus, there was only one time and that time was now. The eternal now of faith. What is fundamentally true about the Christian faith is that God's invitation to life is extended to every human being in the now of time, right here, right now, right on the edge of moment-by-moment time. A divine punch line resides in the universe. There is comedy and laughter and forgiveness because God is *for*, not against, but radically *for* the intensification of joy in human experience. Moreover, when we experience joy, so does God. And of course the opposite is true. When we are weighted down by either perfection (regardless of the form it takes) or by self-righteousness (again, regardless of the form it takes, and it has many), then God experiences unutterable sadness.

Running the risk of overstatement, I would contend that there is a clearer choice regarding religious faith in the twenty-first century. No longer are the issues Methodist versus Presbyterian, Baptist versus Lutheran, or even Catholic versus Protestant. In a certain way, such labels are growing more and more obsolete, though I respect the heritage inherent in each of these religious traditions. What does matter, however, is the posture, the orientation, the overarching sense of faith that a person can discover in his or her life. Is faith a fundamental system of rules? Is scripture a literal answer book? Is each day some kind of perverse divine test? Is there an end-time cosmic reckoning? Is there a right system, a correct system, an orthodox system of faith that must be followed? Is God the big man in the sky, all-knowing, all-controlling, and therefore the one who is to be feared? Or are there turning points in faith that provide a larger hope, not only for the church but also for the world?

Is there another posture toward faith that makes faith an adventure, an exploration, a journey? Is there a way to experience faith as a relationship with God, with the world, with others, with the deepest self? Is there a way to understand that God lives inside the recesses of heart, mind, body, and soul, and therefore, to open the heart is to open up to the divine energy of the world? Is there a way of understanding that the only path to God is ultimately the path that opens the heart? Not a matter of being right or correct, but faith as the experience of living with the presence of God. And is there a way to see faith as a liberating experience, generating great energies of joy and love and compassion, and consequently, the releasing of those energies into the world for the healing of others? And is there a way to understand faith as the ultimate connector to others, building bridges instead of walls toward people of different faiths and backgrounds, believing that there is a common religious energy underneath all specific expressions of religion?

I've tried to figure out why Suzanne made such an unforgettable impression on me. Maybe it's because I've seen so many people like her throughout my years as a minister. Nice people. Good people. People for whom religion had become more regiment than relationship. But upon closer observation, and frankly, a more personal and painful observation, I have to admit that Suzanne is important to me because I see myself in Suzanne. Her struggle has been my struggle, and like most personal struggles, it's probably not finished. Nevertheless, there is a joyful possibility that resonates within my deepest experience of God; it is an assurance that God is about grace and love, about forgiveness and healing, about hope and possibility. There is a ground floor to all of life, and the ground floor of faith is ultimately grace. That, of course, is where real living begins, not in our grand achievements, but in our grateful acceptance.

Several months ago I read a little book by the novelist Reynolds Price, who recounts a time in 1955 when he was a graduate student in Europe. It was the first time he had ever spent Christmas alone. He tells the story of being in Rome on Christmas day, and though on the surface that sounds thrilling and exciting, when you're twenty-two years old and away from home for the very first time, it's not so exciting. He was sitting on a bench outside the colosseum in Rome, and though he had seen the historical sights, he was in fact feeling sorry for himself, sinking down into that river of loneliness and self-pity. But then something happened, and though it was almost fifty years ago, he writes about it with such freshness that it sounds as if it happened yesterday.

He writes, "A young woman, maybe my age, in a tan dress, a coarse brown shawl on her hair and shoulders, one hand on the child beside her—a boy with filthy knees and a coat so tattered it hung in comical strips. Was he five years old or older? They were beggars surely but—no—their hands didn't reach out toward me, though their black eyes never flinched from my face...I knew I had a handful of change...but before I brought it to daylight...the woman shook her head once—No. She gave the boy a gentle push forward...They were selling souvenirs, likely fakes. I smiled a 'No, grazie,' holding both my hands out empty...but the boy reached up and laid the coin in my right palm.

"I'd spent hours with a boyhood coin box; and when I turned the bronze coin over, I knew it was real with the profile of one of the saner Caesars, Hadrian—worth maybe fifteen dollars. I still didn't need it and offered it back. But the child wasn't selling. He returned and trotted off to his mother...She launched a smile of amazing light at me and said what amounted to 'You, for you. The coin is for you.'"

Price ends his little reflection with one simple sentence, "I still have the coin."[2]

What is the Christian faith about if it is not about that one who radically, graciously, generously waits to give to us? Jesus was born to love, and we were born to receive that love. We are all stumbling through the dark, stumbling alone through our years and experiences and insecurities, through our hurts and hopes and dreams. But there is one who waits. Patiently. Steadfastly. All we can do is open our empty hands. We offer neither our goodness nor anything remotely resembling perfection. Just empty hands. All we can do is listen for that voice that says, "You, you, for you." All we can do is clutch love in the palms of our hands.

CHAPTER FOUR

The Heart Aches to Open

When we dare to risk pain—our own, another's, the pain we share—love casts out fear. That is how it works. Love casts out fear, and pain becomes manageable, a part of life and not nearly the most dominant part. Most important of all, when we walk toward our pain, not away from it, we walk hand in hand with others, hesitant sometimes but no longer fearful, for life is strong, strong enough to cast fear from our hearts.

FORREST CHURCH[1]

When I was fifteen years old, I had a religious experience. I started attending the youth group meetings of a very conservative, very fundamentalist church. I didn't know anything about Christian fundamentalism and the literalism of the Bible at the age of fifteen. All I knew then was that these leaders took an interest in me, and they were passionate about the Bible. They found answers in the Bible. They explained to me that there was a simple, overarching story of faith. True faith. Real faith. And, of course, the one and only faith. For them, all the pieces of the Bible fit together like a puzzle. To believe in one piece of the puzzle was to believe in every piece of the puzzle. Only later would I learn that to reject one piece of the puzzle meant the entire structure fell apart as if imploded by a stick of dynamite.

For whatever reasons, reasons I'm probably still not sure of, I came to believe in this buttoned-down presentation of the Christian faith. Maybe it was security. Maybe it was an odd form of teenage rebellion. Other kids smoked cigarettes, drank cheap beer, and explored the world of their sexuality when they were in high school. I became religious. This particular expression of religious faith meant, of course, that I was right and everyone else was wrong. Unless, of course, you happened to belong to this particular church. It meant that I interpreted the Bible in a literalistic way. It meant that I put my feelings on hold, because I was told feelings couldn't be trusted. It meant I put my intellect on hold, because I was warned that using my mind would lead to rationalizing religious ideas, thus undermining the true nature of faith. It's a chilling thought to me now that two of the most important dimensions of the "beautiful self" mentioned by Nouwen—intellect and feeling— were diminished in my adolescent years of faith. It's not that I just started going to church. It was much more than that. I bought into an entire rigorous, one-dimensional system of religion. For a few years this church became my community. But the community was highly conditional, extended only to those who were willing to live within the small, confining, simple little room of Christian fundamentalism.

I'm guessing this is why Suzanne's life became so significant to me. Her stuff was my stuff. I saw her sitting there Sunday after Sunday, but the pain I perceived in her was also my own pain. The ache I felt was my own memory. I know what it's like to have a religion that closes the heart. I suspect some of you reading this book know what it's like as well. A lot of us are recovering from religion! I was weighted down with a God far too heavy to carry and a faith far too disconnected from my deepest self. I was afraid of not being good enough. Afraid of not being worthy enough. The very faith that should have brought healing to my soul only reinforced an intrinsic brokenness I had carried since childhood—the fear of not being good enough for the world.

There are many life experiences that have the power to close the heart. The tragic loss of a loved one. A devastating illness. The loss of a job. The painful ending of a relationship. But what I continue to learn is that living with heart is not a matter of being good enough or sincere enough or even devoted enough. That's the good news. Nor is it about being smart enough or enlightened enough. Maybe even better news. Living with an open heart is about assuming a posture of openness toward life made possible by the gracious openness of God. The God who is like the father jumping off the porch ready to welcome a prodigal son back home. The God who is like a woman sweeping the house looking for that one lost coin. The God who is like the desert nomad wandering and wandering until a new land is found. Living with an open heart means we are willing to answer an invitation from the heart to the heart, that has always been the larger hope of the Christian faith.

Does the heart send us messages? I believe it does. Our hearts are constantly sending messages to our lives. But will we listen? Will we find the courage and openness to listen to our own hearts? Is there a deeper music to be heard in life? Yes. Is there a better landscape to be viewed in life? The answer is yes. To see the world with the heart is to see a whole new world, nothing less than what the Bible calls a "new heaven and new earth." This is spirituality, finding new ways of seeing the world and, most importantly, seeing ourselves.

I made a decision. I'm not exactly sure when I made it. I just don't remember. My sense is that it grew gradually, like slowly walking upon a medieval prayer labyrinth, but it was a clear decision to change directions with my faith. Here are the choices: I would either live with a completely open heart toward the universe, dancing with a different kind of faith and a different kind of God and a different kind of church experience, or I would have no faith at all. In choosing the former, relationships replace regiment. Falling in love with God replaces explanation of God. My personal experiences of the divine become at least as important as the recorded experiences about God found in the Bible. Trust embraces mystery. Feelings sit down with thoughts. My body becomes as important as my soul. And the whole point of my living becomes neither adherence to a religious system nor achievement of God's favor, but the experience of grace, sweet, wonderful, amazing grace that has the power to make the heart glad and heal the deepest wounds of the soul.

I continue to be surprised at how my past experiences— and all the emotions associated with them—lurk within the shadow regions of my soul. Maybe you find that to be true, too. You can be having a great day when suddenly, like a shooting star ripping across the night sky, your spouse will say something and for a moment, for a brief, painful, memory-jogging moment, you hear a critical voice from the past, or you have that feeling you must be a bad person, or you have that terrible emotion of not being good enough. Or I see a Suzanne sitting in the sanctuary of the church, and her very posture signals to me my own struggle to open up to my deepest feelings, or I hear her ask me in the hallway of the church something as wooden as "Why don't you preach more Bible sermons?" and suddenly the whole experience becomes like a huge thunderous voice from my past, rattling the windows of my soul, and even though I know at a rational level that I am more than my history, I can never be less than my history, and what happens is that my old wounds are picked open only to scar over again and again.

The philosopher Alfred North Whitehead conceptualized human experience as an ocean wave. At any given moment in our point-by-point existential living, our history—not some of it, but all of it—is pouring into the present moment of our experience. This is like the swelling energy of a great wave, but as the wave climaxes and folds into the ocean, a new wave is created. And then another. And then another. Thus, the past is forever opening up, pressing into the future, and the waves go on and on and on. Whitehead's viewpoint is refreshingly hopeful, precisely because he understood the work of God as taking the past of any given present moment, full and ripe with history, and then reshaping it into the highest relevant possibility for the future. The past is real. But so is novelty. And creativity. And hope for the future. God is in the business of new creation.

What I believe to be profoundly true about God—woven into my faith and not merely a belief—is the idea that God offers a future, regardless of the past, to the person willing to open up his or her heart.

Fear is often behind the closing of the heart. I look back on my teenage religious experience and question: Was I afraid of my adolescent sexual feelings? Was I afraid of making a transition from my adolescent world to an adult world filled with ambiguity and complexity? Did I have an inkling my parents' marriage was unraveling after twenty years; consequently, was I turning to a religion with all the answers for an uncertain family life? And then I wonder about Suzanne; what was Suzanne afraid of Sunday after Sunday? Why did she need such a black-and-white faith? Why did she need God to be the answer man like the wizard of Oz, the wizard that was no wizard, veiled only by a curtain, more in the imagination than in the reality of the world? Natural fear has its place, to be sure, but the kind of faith that wants to preserve a perfect, chaos-free world, regardless of how artificial it might be, is in the end damaging to the soul.

Isn't fear behind the judgment of others? How else can you explain the irrational hatred toward gays and lesbians or people of different color or religion? What was the driving force behind the 1998 crucifixion, and I don't use that word lightly, of a young, gay college student in Laramie, Wyoming? Matthew Shepard was murdered because of irrational, ugly fear. What motivated two brothers to burn down Jewish synagogues in Sacramento, California, in the summer of 1999? It was fear. What was behind the tragic shootings at Columbine High School? Surely, it was the lethal combination of despair and anger and fear. Why was James Byrd dragged through a Texas town and murdered if it was not white fear?

Ultimately, fear is behind all prejudice, all racism, all sexism, all classism. Fear fuels the fire of all heavy-handed moralism. Fear also drives the engine of religious fundamentalism; whether it's Christian or Jewish or Muslim, it's always about fear. How sad it is when fear is a driving force in a church, issuing forth in the judgment and exclusion of others. Part of what the American citizens are dealing with in the aftermath of September 11, 2001, is a backlash of irrational fear toward people of the Muslim faith, many of them American citizens, many of them as shocked and horrified by the tragedies in New York City and Washington, D.C., as any of us. Yet, just as it would be tragic for fear to close the individual heart, it would be even more tragic for fear to shut the heart of this nation.

I realize now that the adolescent religious experience that captured my imagination years ago was not only a belief in a rigid system of faith, but at a much deeper level, it was my personal deflection of an invitation from the universe to live with an open heart. It was fear. I don't regret that experience from my past, because rarely is that helpful with anything from the past, but I do understand that fear freezes the heart. The songwriter David Gray writes, "It takes a lot of love to keep the heart from freezing."[2] Absolutely true. Sometimes the heart closes with a weighty perfectionism, and sometimes it breaks from personal experiences of wounding. Either way, the heart is closed.

Another singer, writer, poet, David Wilcox, has a wonderful song entitled "Underneath." The refrain captures something of what I'm trying to say:

> But what is it, really, that's keeping me
> from living a life that's true?
> When worries speak louder than wisdom,
> it drowns out all the answers, I knew,
> so I'm tossed on the waves on the surface.
> Still, the mystery's dark and deep,
> with much more frightening stillness…
> underneath.[3]

It's true that opening the heart is mysterious, and not a little scary, but this is exactly what Jesus called upon people to do. Jesus seemed to understand that the pathway to God was always in and through and with the heart. He opened his heart to the lepers, the diseased, those disdained and distanced from society. He opened his heart to the children, even though the disciples thought they were of little consequence to their important activities with Jesus. He opened his heart to the poor, even though many thought they were cursed by God. He opened his heart to people who were non-Jewish, even though he was criticized for doing so. He opened his heart to women, even though they were viewed as second-class citizens during that time and place in history. He opened his heart to his own pain, his own grief, his own feelings of vulnerability, even though then, as now, many tried to enshrine his divinity to the neglect and eclipse of his humanity. Why, after all, would Jesus pray something like, "Let this cup pass from me..." if not for his open-hearted humanity? Jesus understood that the faith experience was not about getting it right or being right or fitting into a right system. Instead, faith was about going underneath, opening the heart, living the adventure, and most of all, experiencing the gracious nod and loving embrace from the God of the universe.

A part of me wanted to reach out to Suzanne as I preached to her week after week, in fact, to all people in churches who have turned faith into a system of rightness more than an authentic adventure of spirituality, and I wanted to say to her that what finally matters is what is underneath. Letting go. Being loved. Opening the heart. But in truth, while I wanted to offer this wondrous reality to Suzanne, I was acutely aware that I needed it myself. Far too often I am driven to accomplish. Far too often I am filled with unrealistic expectations of myself. Far too often I have had unrealistic expectations for those around me, including those I love the most. And far too often I am disappointed with myself, and to a degree, I've wasted much precious energy being disappointed in others. It's not just any heart that aches to open to God's grace, it's my heart and Suzanne's heart. It's true for those who hear sermons. Maybe even more true for those who preach them.

Go with me to the end of Archibald MacLeish's play *J.B.* In the haunting ending of the story, Job has lost everything. Nothing left but wilderness. Job's wife, Sarah, is sitting there with him and notices a twig of forsythia. I love forsythia, which, like daffodils and tulips and crocuses, speaks to us of the promise of something beyond winter, the promise of new life and springtime beyond the emptiness of winter. She is holding a twig of forsythia and she says to him, "Look Job, this forsythia, the first few...petals...I found it growing in the ashes, gold as though it did not know…You wanted justice and there was none—only love."

Job says to his wife, "God does not love. God is."

She replies, "But we do. [We love.] That's the wonder."

And then she admits to him that at a certain point all the wilderness had become so overpowering that she briefly thought about taking her own life. But then she says, "Oh, I never could! Even the forsythia…" she says half laughing, half crying, "even the forsythia could stop me."

Job and Sarah then cling to each other, peering at the darkness inside the door. That's often how the heart feels when it has closed shut. Just darkness, so dark we don't know the way, can't find the way, can't see the way. It's a darkness that Jesus would eventually know, too.

Job says to her, "It's too dark to see."

And then Sarah says, "Then blow on the coals of my heart, my darling…Blow on the coals of my heart."[4]

I know, and you know too, what it means to close the heart. It's the human journey that not even Jesus could escape. But why would he want to escape it? It's in this human journey that we find the great treasure of ourselves and God and one another. Yet, there is a love, a crowbar of love that is forever coming close, trying to pry open the doors of our heart. Yes, God comes close to you and me in the midst of our darkness. And what I find is that most of the time, not all the time, but most of the time God comes close to us through one another, and we blow on the coals of one another's hearts. A miracle happens. A miracle in our heart of darkness. There is warmth and there is light. How the heart aches for such a miracle that is at the center of Christianity.

CHAPTER FIVE

Welcoming the Stranger Home

*When, bubbling up from deep within us, we hear a voice
calling us back to our dreams, we feel compelled, despite our
fears, to listen...the beat we must follow now is our own
heartbeat, that mortal drum beckoning us to rediscover the
immortal rhythm of our deeper selves, which some call the
soul.*

MARK GERZON[1]

John Mellencamp grew up in Seymour, Indiana, just a few
miles from my hometown of Salem. Although he was reared
in a strict fundamentalist household, rock-and-roll music pulsed
through his body, combusting into a wild energy of creativity
and rebellion. He loved his guitar. He loved his music. And he
dreamed of making it big. But how do you make it big? Well,
when you're a teenager trying to get out of Seymour, Indiana,
you imitate those rock groups already making their appearance
on the record charts and enjoying the spotlight on Dick Clark's
American Bandstand. That's exactly what Mellencamp did. He
copied someone else's voice.

44

And he did pretty well. In fact, he landed a record contract or two. But he was repeatedly told that with a name like *Mellencamp*, he would never sell records. And so some marketing moron made him change his name—a final indignity—John Mellencamp became Johnny Cougar.

One by one the records came out, but they met with only modest success. He left Los Angeles. Wandered back home again to Indiana. But this time he came back home to listen to his life, to reconnect with his roots and rediscover his own experience. Suddenly, John Mellencamp began to discover that what he needed to write about was his own life. He wrote about small-town life in southern Indiana. Wrote about hot, sexy, small-town teenagers like "Jack and Diane, grow'n up in the heartland." And when the bottom dropped out of the economy for the family farmer, Mellencamp sang about "blood on the scarecrow."

What he discovered was that his genius had been with him all along. In some ways, it wouldn't be an exaggeration to call what happened to him a miracle. John Mellencamp booted Johnny Cougar off the face of the Earth. He would either be himself, find his own voice, live his own life, or it wouldn't happen at all. He allowed his music to be his life, and his life his music.

If faith in God is about anything that is real and substantial within the human experience, then it must surely be about finding our true selves. There is a world of difference between faith *in* ourselves and a faith *of* ourselves. The true object of faith is always God. No argument there. But true faith is always a song that emerges from ourselves, belonging to the depth and authenticity of our own lives. And if it is true that God lives within the depths of the human experience, living in that deepest place of the human heart, then faith is not a matter of putting ourselves on hold as much as it is finding our true selves and, in turn, finding God.

I think of many turning points within my faith experience, but none is more powerful than the commitment of listening to my own life. It's the adventure of finding a faith that radically belongs to me. Not to my parents. Not to the church. Not to my peers. Not to my seminary professors. Not even a faith that belongs to a book as important as the Bible. Genuine faith is finding the courage to open the heart and move into our most authentic lives. In some ways, living in a world that is stressed-out, stretched-out beyond belief, one of the great values of faith for the twenty-first century is its power to quiet the soul and give us permission to listen once again to our hearts. The English priest George Herbert wrote years ago, "Love bade me welcome; yet my soul drew back."[2] That is the religious struggle in a nutshell, the heart bidding us home and our struggle to say yes.

We have just one opportunity to live the gift of our lives. This is not a dress rehearsal. To miss it, to squander the potential of the soul, full of wonderful light and palpable shadow, is to make a mistake of the worst kind. Religion, rather than obscuring this awesome task of living, should actually help us move closer and closer to the genuine core of our essence. Unfortunately, in so many different ways, religion has oppressed the flowering of the soul. Guilt and shame do it. Heavy-handed moralism does it. Conformity within highly structured religious communities can do it. Biblical literalism that locates the energy of faith within a book rather than the heart can do it. Substituting meaningful reflection with religious busyness can do it. Focusing on the second coming of Jesus while at the same time missing the implications of the first coming of Jesus can do it. And behind it all, fear can do it.

Faith is at its best when it moves people deeper and deeper into their autobiographical odyssey. Not living someone else's life. Not following someone else's dream. It is the sacred process of writing our own story. This is why worship and prayer are so important to the faith experience. When I pray, I'm not just submitting my "to do" list to God. I'm pausing to listen to my deepest needs, and in so doing I begin to experience God's presence mingling in the most intimate place of the heart. When I pray for another person, it simply means I am holding another person in the deepest place of my soul. That's where prayers come from, after all, they come from the most sacred center of human consciousness. When I worship, truly worship in the context of music, sacred symbols, and rich architecture, I am at one and at the same time transcending myself while moving closer to myself. Or in the words of Jesus, the very minute I begin to lose myself in God is the very minute I begin to find myself in God.

Maybe a story will help. Noted author Parker Palmer describes a critical time in his life when he was approached by a small college to become their next president. By most standards, becoming a president of a college has a certain ring of prestige to it, hard work to be sure, but there are some rewards to it as well. He went on the interview, talked with the trustees, and on the side it was signaled to him that he was the candidate they wanted and that the job was his if he wanted it. Parker Palmer is a Quaker. In the Quaker tradition, if you are going to make a major life decision, what you do is talk with other Quakers, discern the process, and wait for the deepest wisdom of God to rise to the surface. (Probably wouldn't hurt any of us to practice a little Quaker discernment.)

Like a lot of us, Palmer decided that he knew what he wanted, he assumed that what he wanted was what God wanted, and so he went through the process wanting more confirmation than he did discernment from his Quaker friends. It was one of those situations similar to when a good friend looks at me and says, "Now, Scott, are you really wanting feedback, or do you want me just to agree with you?" (I hate it when that happens!)

Listen to how Parker Palmer describes his listening process. "For a while, the questions were easy, at least for a dreamer like me: What is your vision for the institution? What is its mission in the larger society? How would you change the curriculum?...But about halfway into the process, someone asked a question that sounded easier, yet it turned out to be very hard: What would you like most about being president?"

He said he lowered his head. He could feel his heart throbbing. And then it took him over a minute to make any kind of response. Sometimes sixty seconds can last forever. Slowly he started to say that he would hate to give up his writing and teaching, and that he would not really like all the politics of running a school and all the fund-raising that goes with it, and that he would hate giving up his summers. He mumbled on like that until the person who had asked the question in the first place said, "Parker, may I remind you that I asked what you would most *like*?" He said, "Oh yes, I'm getting to that. I'm getting to that answer," and he continued this sullen litany of things that he didn't want to do as a college president. Finally— moment of truth—he said to the committee in the smallest voice he had ever used, "Well, I guess what I'd like most is getting my picture in the paper with the word *president* under it."[3]

Oh, how laughable it is. When I first read that story, I started to giggle. And then I laughed. Then I underlined it. And then I read it again. And then I quit giggling and laughing. Because I realized that I, and maybe you too, have made some decisions with my own life, decisions that betrayed the fundamental core of my life story, and at times I did it with motivations just as laughable as Parker's. There he was with those respected Quakers, friends who knew him and loved him, and that's all he could come up with, a picture in the paper. Thankfully they did not laugh. He recounts that there was the longest, most awkward, most gut-wrenching silence. Then someone finally worked up enough nerve and quietly asked, "Parker, can you think of an easier way to get your picture in the paper?"

There are so many ways of deflecting the true discovery of the inner self, not the least of which is the use of religion. This, however, runs against the grain of everything Jesus seemed to be about. He was not trying to get people to become something they were not. Instead, his call was for people to move more deeply into who they really are. Perhaps the word is *restoration*. His energy of love and reality of acceptance created the possibility of restoration for people, people who had lost their way and lost themselves. Thomas Merton captured it well when he wrote, "For me to be a saint means to be myself. Therefore the problem of sanctity and salvation is in fact the problem of finding out who I am and of discovering my true self."[4]

There's a story in the book of Luke about a man who was demon possessed. The Gerasene demoniac. In the ancient world it was believed that invisible flying demons, not unlike germs, were forever buzzing through the sky, at times invading the body of a man or woman, rendering the person broken and marginalized from life. Part of an ecu-faith is to recognize that such a first-century worldview is no longer valid. Demons don't fly through the sky. Demons don't take over human bodies. A centered faith recognizes the difference between the underlying reality of the biblical stories and the forms in which these ancient stories were told. But what we also know, many of us firsthand, is that people do experience painful, if not devastating, brokenness. Sometimes it is over choices we have made. Sometimes it is over choices others have made. Regardless, we know that to be alive is to struggle with hurt and pain and anxiety.

What's fascinating about this story is that Jesus is portrayed as bringing healing to the man, this man who wandered aimlessly among the tombs, broken, chaotic, tortured by his own deadness. Emanating from Jesus was a love-energy, a grace-energy that restored the man to his right mind. He rediscovered life, his own life, and that discovery goes to the heart of the Christian faith. To me, one of the saddest presentations of the Christian faith is that line of reasoning that suggests conversion is becoming something we are not. I think it is just the opposite. I think God wants us to be converted, if you will, but converted back to our true, original goodness. It's this inner self, this inner child that longs for nurture and love and expression.

I am moved by Derek Walcott's poem "Love After Love" because it portrays this sense of opening the heart to our very selves. Unless we can open our hearts to ourselves, there's little chance we'll be able to open them for others. Little chance we will open them to God. Both the generosity and generativity of Walcott's poem are expressed through the sacramental images of bread and wine and feasting at a table. Christian images to be sure.

The time will come
when with elation,
you will greet yourself arriving
at your own door, in your own mirror,
and each will smile at the other's welcome,
and say, sit here. Eat.
You will love again the stranger who was your self.
Give wine. Give bread. Give back your heart
to itself, to the stranger who has loved you
all your life, whom you ignored

for another, who knows you by heart.
Take down the love letters from the bookshelf,
the photographs, the desperate notes,
peel your own image from the mirror.
Sit. Feast on your life.[5]

I read this poem and I turn it over again and again, like turning over dirt in the garden, preparing for the planting of tomatoes or basil or eggplant. Something wants to grow in this poem. What do you hear? What do you feel inside the images? What does the language do to you?

I'm drawn to the word *elation*. Such a powerful word. Quieter than *celebration,* more subtle than *happiness,* more evocative than *joy,* this word *elation* moves me inward, toward the deeper places of my soul. I think about how rare elation is in my life. Think about it. When is the last time you experienced any elation? This is not entertainment or a superficial good time. This isn't Las Vegas. Elation only happens when we join the inner world with the outer world. Oh, and that image of *giving back the heart to itself.* That is remarkable. It's not so much that the heart disappears as it is that the heart gets lost. There is a hospitality our soul wants to give the heart. A welcome. A reunion. A homecoming. And the whole experience becomes a moment of communion. Hmm…the heart that is welcomed home is a sacramental moment. Grace and mystery touching the soul. This must have been something of the experience for that Gerasene demoniac. There is elation but it's calming. Almost subdued, but clearly joyful. And then the *love letters.* And then the *photographs.* Memory. Painful memories? Sad memories? Happy memories? Yes to all three. Something has been lost in our lives. Not forgotten, but almost forgotten. Remembered enough, however, so that when the heart is welcomed home, the heart knows it's home, feels itself at home.

It seems to me that opening the heart is not exactly the same as self-discovery. It goes deeper than self-improvement. This isn't just a matter of finding a new life strategy. To open the heart, listening to the deepest voices of the self, is a sacred process. A lifelong pilgrimage toward that place within us called home. It is called God. It is called depth. It is called Christ; not

Christ as in a person, but Christ as an energy that is waiting to be stirred within us all. To move toward it is what it means to be religious—to stir up the Christ, that is true faith.

Again, this is why I resist presentations of the Christian faith suggesting the primary experience of faith is the mandatory denial of the self. I don't want to overstate it. There is a place for self-discipline and improving the self. But for the most part, the denial of the self as a concept has been a destructive one for Christians. It's the idea, found in almost all American Protestantism, that what is needed is a severe denouncement of the sinful, shameful, wretched self. There is brokenness within all of us, including myself, or better said, especially in myself. But my brokenness is present precisely because I have refused to welcome my heart home. Instead of turning away from my deepest self, God is inviting me to sit and eat, to open my heart and welcome the stranger home. That is elation. That is the cosmic hospitality that beats in the heart of God.

Not long ago I was waiting to pick up my son Matthew at the airport, and while I was waiting, I started to notice all the other people who were there waiting for friends or family or maybe business associates. But what made the waiting especially interesting was that, because of a variety of weather delays, the waiting was taking place at two o'clock in the morning. The world is different at two o'clock in the morning; it is a quiet kind of waiting. Many of us were a little bleary-eyed, and our bodies were sagging a bit from fatigue, but no one was complaining, no one was angry, we were all, well, we were all just waiting.

I couldn't help but notice a couple of men dressed nicely in black suits who were also waiting, and while they waited they held up cards with names on them. I've seen this hundreds of times before at airports. I'm sure you have too. A driver is waiting to pick up a client for a company or maybe a special guest for some kind of significant event. What I noticed, however, is that most of us were roaming and shifting, doing anything to break the boredom, but not these men in the black suits. Instead, they stood almost at attention, they stood straight and dignified as if each one had a two-by-four running from the top of his neck all the way down to the soles of his feet. If they were utterly bored like the rest of us who were standing around and waiting, they sure didn't show it, because they just kept waiting and waiting and waiting.

What I noticed is that every time someone walked through the door of the gate, they would hold up their signs just a little bit higher, and it would say something like MARK BROWN or JOHN SMITH or KAREN JOHNSON. They didn't know exactly what the person would look like or what they would be like or what they would sound like, but that didn't matter, because they were there to find someone, and so they waited and waited and waited. Finally, when the plane started to empty out and a steady stream of weary travelers were making their way through the door of the gate, they would try to make eye-contact with every passenger, trying to find any glimmer of recognition, some expression on the face that would say, "This is it! I'm looking for you! You're looking for me! We belong together!"

As I watched those men in the black suits waiting and the passengers stumbling through the door of the gate in the dark, gloomy hours of the middle of the night, I thought to myself, *Could it be, could it be that God is looking for you and looking for me like that? Could it be that God is searching for me in a way that is unlike any other time in my life? Could it be that God is holding up a sign with my name on it, your name on it—first name, middle name, last name—and God is waiting with infinite patience and perseverance, waiting for some glimpse on our part, some faint recognition on our part, waiting for some nod, some smile, some signal from us that says, "Yes, yes we have found one another, welcome home!"*

Someone is looking for you. And someone is looking for me. Yes, we are on a pilgrimage, but more importantly, God is on a pilgrimage, and God has been looking for us, longing for us; God has been waiting even into the dark, foggy hours of the middle of the night in hope that through some faint glimmer of recognition we might find one another. There is something in the universe seeking us.

You are no accident. I am no accident. We want to reconnect with our sense of destiny. We want to find our deeper selves. We want to believe in our future. We want to believe that there is some *one*, some *thing*, some *energy*—we call it God, but we could also call it hope or love or awe or wonder or mystery or meaning, we could even call it Christ—but there is someone waiting for you, and maybe that someone has been waiting for you all your life, waiting for you even in the middle of the night, and that someone is holding up a sign. And guess what? Your name is on that sign. God is waiting. Waiting to welcome us home to ourselves.

CHAPTER SIX

The Soul Longs for Healing

The act of entering into the mysteries of the soul, without sentimentality or pessimism, encourages life to blossom forth according to its own designs and with its own unpredictable beauty. Let us imagine care of the soul, then, as an application of poetics to everyday life.

THOMAS MOORE[1]

Faith is not about preserving a system of faith. Systems and denominations and doctrines may be helpful, and to some extent necessary, in the faith experience, but to elevate them to a goal or destination in and of themselves is a mistake. The temptation is always to confuse the explanation of faith with the experience of faith. What I continue to find as a turning point in my own spiritual journey is that there is a difference as wide as the Grand Canyon between explaining God at a rational level and experiencing God at a soulful level. Not to be overlooked, one of the hallmark characteristics of American Protestantism is the use of reason in understanding faith, and I think reason is essential to faith; at the same time, it's important that faith not become mere rationalism. What's needed is a theology soaked in the red blood of human experience. Not unlike the life of Jesus.

Faith is about touching the numinous, the holy, the sacred. Faith is about touching the mystery of love and the beauty of grace pulsing through the world. It's about touching and being touched by the healing presence of God. The human soul is thirsty for a direct experience of God, not just hearing about it or thinking about it or reading about it. It is the spiritual experience that the soul desires because when it happens, when it draws as near to us as living inside our own body, the human soul finds itself at home and blossoms into its beautiful, wonderful, marvelous wholeness.

As I mentioned earlier, religion is not perfection. Not even the pursuit of perfection. I was reading not long ago about the apple industry in the state of Washington and their misguided pursuit of growing the perfect apple. For years, apples grown in Washington were considered some of the best anywhere. What happened, however, is that the farmers tried to develop the perfect looking apple. Perfectly shaped. Perfectly red. Perfectly shiny. And that's exactly what they did. Unfortunately, the more perfect the apples appeared, the more tasteless they became. The apple industry in Washington is now suffering because they created the perfectly *tasteless* apple. In the same way, faith is not about being perfectly tasteless or morally sanitized or doctrinally correct. Measuring up is not the name of the game. Spiritual wholeness is a feeling of walking through the world as a complete and whole human being, flawed to be sure, but nevertheless whole. The poet Rumi once wrote, "I will meet you in a field out beyond all right doing and wrong doing."[2] That's the place where we encounter God.

One of the most basic ideas associated with the Christian faith is that we are all sinners and in need of God's grace. I want to be careful here because I think there is a certain truth to that idea. Yet I find myself questioning why human sinfulness has to be the beginning place for our relationship with God. Why does the pathway to God have to be paved with the stones of personal failure and sinfulness? Is it the case that grace can only be amazing when we are convinced of our personal wretchedness? Or is there another way? Why not let the path toward God be paved with God's deepest desire? God's deepest love? God's deepest passion for each and every human being to be a whole person? Many of us know firsthand that a relationship with another person based upon personal neediness is rarely a healthy relationship. Healthy relationships happen when two people want to be with one another, when they desire to bring their dreams and strengths to one another. Couldn't the same be said of our relationship with God? We have a relationship with God, not so much because we need God, but because we want God. Even so, there will always be that element of personal sinfulness or, as I prefer to think of it, personal brokenness. Yet brokenness is far different in feeling, in tone, than sinfulness. I don't deny that people sin. At times we all have to come to grips with sinful, and at times even evil, decisions that we have made. But all sin emerges from the broken, fractured, fragmented state of a person's reality.

The greatest need we have, therefore, is not punishment from above but healing from within, and that's where the grace of God begins to touch our lives. I use the word *healing* with a bit of trepidation given the fact that there are certain connotations around the word that are less than helpful. I'm not talking about that cable television, sweaty evangelist, people-fainting-on-the-stage sense of the word *healing*. Rather, taking my cue from Jesus, I'm suggesting that what he understood was that people were and are desperate for a kind of healing, a kind of grace in their lives. Healing in the sense of restoration to the human spirit. Healing in the sense of renewal of the human heart. Healing in the sense of revival of hope for the human adventure. What Jesus knew how to do so well was to bring joy to people in the midst of their pain, relief to people in the midst of their pressures, grace to people in the midst of their harsh and demanding lives. He could even speak a word, and with one well-chosen word he could immediately bring life to people. Jesus seemed to know, as do all great religious leaders, that the deepest need of every human being is not more information or more knowledge or more steps for a better life. And certainly the last thing people need from God is punishment over poor decisions. What we need is healing for the deepest wounds of life.

I want to take a closer look at a biblical story I alluded to earlier, primarily because it illustrates the nature of God embodied in the life of Jesus. Found in the gospel of Luke, it's the story of Jesus healing the Gerasene demoniac. The central figure of the drama is described as a man who lived among the tombs. Symbolic of the fact that you can be alive and still be dead. Symbolic of the fact that you can eat and sleep and still be dead. Symbolic of the fact that you can work and play and go to church every Sunday and still be dead. You can even preach sermons and write books and still be spiritually dead.

But more than living among the dead, this man also ran among the tombs naked. Sometimes in the Bible nakedness is a sign of innocence, as in the story of the garden of Eden, but in this story nakedness symbolizes that which is vulnerable. This was a man marginalized by society. And if all of that isn't enough, this man was radically, utterly, absolutely tormented within himself. He was dangerous to himself. Dangerous to others. The people in the little village tried to use ropes and chains to keep the man under control, just to keep him in his place, which was no place at all. This is a story not unlike Mary Shelley's *Frankenstein.* Nobody wanted to look at this man. Nobody wanted to speak to this man. He lived in a faceless world, and there's only one thing worse than having everybody stare at you; it's having no one look at you at all.

My first inclination after reading the story is to dismiss the whole thing. After all, isn't it really just a little too dramatic? Sure, there are people in our society who are tormented like this man. People who are mentally ill and tortured like this man. But for the most part, the story feels exaggerated, leaving the impression that this man may have been in a bad way, but such a condition has not–nor will it ever–happened to me. Yet just at the moment I'm ready to discount the entire story, I find a turning point. Actually, two very simple lines that become turning points in the story, and thus turning points that define the Christian faith.

Jesus looks at the man. The face of Jesus turns toward the man at the exact time when everyone else turns away from the man. Jesus turns toward the man and asks him: "What is your name?" I find myself lingering with that line. "What is your name?" I can't help but wonder, what is *your* name, you who are reading this book right now, what *is* your name? What is *my* name, this man sitting at a desk pounding the keys of a computer, thinking of the next sentence, thinking of the next thought, wondering if what he is writing will connect with another human being? What is *my* name when I walk along Madison Avenue in New York, or *my* name when I walk along the beach in California, or what is *my* name after I utter harsh words to my wife or wake in the middle of the night and cannot go back to sleep because I am worried about my daughter? Our name is the most personal, most intimate link between our inner world and outer world. The name means the person. The name means our essence. Therefore, for Jesus to address the name of this man is for Jesus to address the depth of this man's brokenness. One essential dimension of the Christian faith is that God is found at the very place where divine healing and human brokenness encounter one another.

It's true that Jesus came to jump-start the kingdom of God, God's rule and activity in the world, but what is behind that word *G-O-D*? *God*, that word *God* means the ground of all reality, the deepest source of life and meaning and joy residing in every human being; the word *God* means that source of all creative, transforming love existing in the universe. But what Jesus does in that one question so succinctly posed to the demon-possessed man is to take the concept of God and put a face on it. "What is your name?" That is to say, even though God is the ground of all being and the source of all creativity, even though God is greater than anything that can be conceived of in the human mind, in that one question—"What is your name?"—Jesus imparts the genius of inspiration: God cares about you. God relates to you. God suffers with you. God wants to heal you.

Not long ago my mother died. Her name was Joyce. That was her name. Her name was Joyce. I've learned a lot in the days since her death. On the one hand, my mother's death is nothing compared to the depth and breadth of tragedy in the world. It's nothing compared to the big problems of AIDS in Africa or poverty among children in our own country or racism that continues to plague our twenty-first century world. My mother's passing is nothing compared to the losses some of the people in my own congregation have experienced, deep losses, tragic losses, losses that leave you as numb and wordless as the Rock of Gibraltar. Mothers die every day.

On the other hand, what I've learned since my mother's death is that brokenness is brokenness, and sadness is sadness, and fear is fear, and grief is grief, and heartache is heartache, and confusion is confusion. Whether it belongs to a tormented man running among the dead centuries ago or whether it belongs to me personally or whether it belongs to you in your personal situation, it really doesn't matter. Because what matters the most is that there is a face of Jesus that says to me in my situation and to you in your situation–"What is your name?" And that is one of the most radical dimensions of the Christian gospel. God has a healing posture toward the world.

I don't believe in a God who fixes things. That's the problem with some of these stories in the Bible. To be honest, they can easily give you the impression that God is little more than a Mr. Fix-It up in the sky. Without a doubt, many in the ancient world thought of God in that way. I know a lot of people in churches today who continue to think that way. But when I go under the surface of the story, what I find is not a "fix-it" God, but a "healing" God. There's a big difference between fixing a human life and healing a human life, just as there is a big difference between curing a person and healing a person. I've often wondered: *Maybe this demon-possessed man had been waiting a lifetime for someone to ask him, "What is your name?"* I'm not sure. What I do know is that in that one question, this fragmented human soul came to know that his suffering was not beyond God's love and that his brokenness was not beyond God's touch.

And that's what I've had to learn for myself after the death of my mother. What I've had to learn is that it's all right to believe God wants to bring a little healing into my life in the midst of my loss. That it's okay to cancel a few appointments. That it's okay to let some other people care for me. It's the reaching out to one another that matters. It's the gift of friendship that carries the energy of healing. Nobody fixed me after the death of my mother, and nobody, including God, can fix you either. But God has and is and will provide healing for people, and in a metaphoric kind of way, maybe it all begins with that one penetrating question, "What is your name?" Because another way of saying it is that no matter the depth or breadth of our suffering, God embraces and holds and clings to our lives.

Jesus asked the man, "What is your name?"

"Hmm...I'll tell you what my name is, Jesus, my name is *Legion.*"

Play on words. "My name is *Legion* because *we are many.*" A reference to the fact that this man was tormented by a thousand different problems, surely a sign that there were multiple demons inside the man. But even backing away from the literalization of the story, isn't it, in a way, true? Aren't *we* Legion? The same demons I see in you, I also, if I'm spiritually honest, see in myself. The very things I despise in another human being are probably closer to the surface of my own life than I want to admit. That's the reason we don't want to see the mentally ill, the reason we don't want to see the homeless, the reason we don't want to see the contorted physical features of another human being; it's because it triggers fears about our own wholeness. Yes, we are Legion, for we are many. It's easier, isn't it, to hate another race rather than face what we hate inside ourselves? It's easier, isn't it, to despise people of other religions rather than face insecurity over our own religion? It's easier, isn't it, to demonize someone else in our family—a mother, a father, a brother, a sister—rather than face the demons inside our own hearts?

Jesus looked at the man and restored his humanity, but the man's first and most immediate impulse was to go home with Jesus. Can you blame him? Any home had to have been better than that old, desolate, give-me-the-heebie-jeebies kind of cemetery where he had been living. Jesus, however, deflects the man's enthusiasm, as if to say, "Great attitude but wrong direction." Jesus wants the man to go back home, back to his family, back to the club, back to work, back to school, back to his relationships. The idea is this: If the healing face of Jesus has looked upon you, then you need to begin to look upon others with that same healing face. He says to the man, "Now, you go back home. You go get a shower. Spend a little money and buy that new suit. I want you to hold your head up high. I want you to smile at people. And here's what I really want you to do: Every chance you get, I want you to tell people how much your faith means to you, you tell them what love and compassion have done for you, you tell them that God specializes in putting back together the broken pieces of men and women. Shattered glass, shattered family, shattered life—doesn't really matter—you tell them what God has done for you." And then Jesus sends the man on his way.

That's the story.

My sense is that we are all looking for some divine face to cast a healing look our way. A face of hope. Compassion. Love. It seems to me that a minimal question that needs to be asked of any presentation of the Christian faith is this: Does this particular expression of faith, the God behind the faith, does that God bring healing to the human spirit? Does that God enhance life? Does that God bring healing to families and cities and communities? Does that God bring healing to a world torn apart by ecological violence? Does that God have the power to heal the scars of racism and sexism and ageism?

I know that in the midst of the recent loss of my mother, I saw all kinds of faces. I saw my own face a little more clearly than I had seen it in the past. I saw more of my grief, not just grief for my mother's passing, but grief over what the relationship never became, grief over my relationship to her and her relationship to me. We loved each other, but like so many, we weren't always good about expressing that love. I saw my face as a little boy as I remembered my mother. I saw my face as a young man as I tried to help my mother through a bewildering time of depression. I saw my face as a middle-aged man saying good-bye to my mother as I shared some thoughts at her funeral.

But I also saw some other faces. I saw some faces of friends I had not seen in years on the day of her burial. My old high school principal came to the funeral, even took me aside and whispered, "You know, we're just a small school but you sure have made us proud." I could have melted into tears. And some old neighbors I had not seen since graduating from high school came to the funeral. A girl with whom I attended kindergarten, who now owns a florist shop in my hometown, took care of all the flowers. She was so sweet and tender. I even saw some faces from my own congregation, people reaching out to help and support me. I didn't ask them for anything. They were just there. And in all of them I saw the healing face of God. It doesn't fix anything; but it can heal everything.

Yes, the face of love and compassion does heal. Such a view of the Christian faith has become for me the essence of faith, a faith that brings us home into the household of all things. It's a faith that brings life. Rather than laboring under the burden of being good enough, righteous enough, spiritual enough, religious enough, it's a faith that finds God saying, "I'm enough. My love is enough. Come home to me and come home to yourself." To be sure, there is something healthy about recognizing our shortcomings and failures, but they are always symptomatic of a larger brokenness in our lives. I'm just not sure that is the beginning place for faith. Instead, the heart of the Christian gospel is that we belong with God and God belongs with us. Such is the gospel of grace, and grace is always enough.

CHAPTER SEVEN

The Power of Hope

It is a weakening and discoloring idea, that rustic people knew God personally once upon a time—or even knew selflessness or courage or literature—but that it is too late for us. In fact, the absolute is available to everyone in every age. There never was a more holy age than ours, and never less.

ANNIE DILLARD[1]

It was both hope and healing I felt as I glanced at a photograph in the newspaper one summer morning not long ago. It was a striking close-up of a woman. She was wearing a wool cap, wisps of blond hair falling down on her forehead. Her face was windblown and burned. Her eyes shut tightly. Large salty tears were streaming down her ruddy cheeks. Her name was Kelly Perkins, and to this day I continue to be amazed at her story.

In November 1995, she was at the UCLA Medical Center dying of a virus that was mysteriously destroying her heart. Doctors made the decision that the only way this young woman could survive would be through a heart transplant. Coincidentally, only a few miles away from the hospital, a forty-year-old woman was thrown from a horse and tragically died that night. What was death for one became life for another. In November of that year Kelly Perkins received the miracle of her new heart.

The next year, merely ten months after her heart transplant, Kelly resumed one of her life passions—hiking in the beautiful California mountains. More than hiking, Kelly and her husband Craig climbed the steep summit of Yosemite's Half Dome. The next year, she did an even more dramatic climb. This time she became the first person with a heart transplant to climb Mount Whitney, more than 14,000 feet in elevation. After that remarkable climb, Kelly was sought after for interviews and newspaper stories; she even appeared on *Good Morning America.*

One of the people who took note of Kelly's story, putting two and two together, was the heart donor's daughter. Amazingly, it was her mother's heart that was beating inside Kelly Perkins' chest. Contact was made. A friendship was established. In the meantime, Kelly was preparing for one more climb. This time her challenge would be Mount Fuji in Japan. Although only 12,000 feet in elevation, Mount Fuji is regarded as a sacred place because of its mystical beauty. Some have claimed that seeing the sunrise from Mount Fuji is one of life's most religious experiences.

Kelly Perkins, 5 feet 3 inches tall, only ninety-five pounds, and possessed with a heart much bigger than the one inside her body, made the arduous ascent, grueling step after grueling step, but she made it. After several difficult hours, she made it to the top of the summit, arriving with her husband and a personal trainer in time to see the glorious, ineffable sunrise on Mount Fuji.

What Kelly didn't know was that her husband was carrying with him a small leather pouch. What she didn't know was that he had made arrangements with the donor's daughter to bring a photograph of her mother. And what she didn't know was that Craig was carrying in that leather pouch the ashes of the woman who gave Kelly back her life. Crouching with Kelly in the lengthening morning sunlight, he told her the complete story. She wept. She wept cold, freezing, salty tears. And that was the photograph I saw in the newspaper. Kelly Perkins wept with gratitude, but more than that, she wept with a sense that this woman whom she had never met, this woman who enabled her to reclaim her life, was indeed a presence with her. Clutching the photograph of her unknown-known donor, Kelly swirled the donor's gray remains into the sky of that magnificent Japanese landscape.

There is nothing more satisfying than when the broken circles of our lives are reconnected. It might not be as dramatic as an ascent upon Mount Fuji, but to heal the wounds and complete the broken circles of our lives means everything in the pursuit of our wholeness. Most of us in one way or another live with the pain of loss, particularly broken circles of relationships that at one time were good, or should have been good but, because of decisions or circumstances or events beyond our control, the circle was broken. These broken circles accumulate inside our lives like ancient ruins in Italy. Broken pieces, sharp edges, each fragment becoming a reminder of another time, another place, a memory of wholeness lost. Yet there is a kind of energy that comes from these ancient ruins. The ruins of our lives are not so much indictments of past failures as they are whispers of hope for our future.

There is perhaps no biblical narrative that better speaks to the reality of hope than the one found in the book of Genesis involving Abraham and Sarah. The narrative begins when God calls them to "Go from your country and your father's house to the land that I will show you. I will make you a great nation, and I will bless you, and make your name great." At this moment a major shift in human understanding takes place. As Thomas Cahill has pointed out in his book *The Gifts of the Jews*, up until this point, reality was understood as circular, people living life upon the great wheel of the gods. But at this moment history is born.[2] And so is journey. And so is hope. No longer passively waiting for the capricious verdict of the gods, Abraham and Sarah are called to go forward, move forth, put one foot in front of the other and believe that God is calling them into a meaningful future.

The context of this journey, at least on the surface, speaks more of death than it does of hope. First of all, there was famine. Literal in that ancient world, but metaphorically the idea of famine speaks to the dryness and deadness and malnutrition of the human spirit that surrounds all of us. And if famine isn't enough, there is also barrenness. Abraham and Sarah could not have children, and though it was an ancient mistake to assume that barrenness was always the fault of the woman, the fact remains that they could not get pregnant and, in turn, they could not secure their future. It's in the face of these circumstances, famine and barrenness, that God calls them into the future, inviting them to believe and trust that God will give them a great land and a great nation to fill the land.

There are two layers to the narrative of Abraham and Sarah, moreover, two layers to our own experience. There are the facts and then there is the story. The story of our lives is the part of us that opens up to feeling, to thoughts, to emotions, to dreams, wounds, and aspirations. Someone might say to you, "I retired last year." That's a fact. But someone might also say, "I feel like a new man since I retired last year." That's the story. "I've been exploring new parts of my personality since I retired last year." That's the story. "I've been kind of depressed since I retired last year." That's the story. "You know, my husband has been driving me crazy since he retired last year." That's part of the story too! There are the facts of our lives and then there is the story of our lives, our thoughts, our feelings, our spiritual yearnings; that's where God works.

Everybody is dealing with their own set of facts and, at some point, everybody has some facts they don't like. Facts they wish they could change but can't. Yet hope happens when a person moves from the facts to the story. The story is the place of faith, for the story is about what you are feeling, and the story is about what you are choosing to believe about yourself and others, the story is what you choose to believe about God. Remember it like this: We deal with the facts; we choose the story.

I recently had what for me was a life highlight. Nobel Peace Prize recipient Elie Wiesel came and spoke at Texas Christian University, and it was my honor to share the podium with him and, in fact, respond to his speech that night. I talked to him. I sat beside him. Had my picture taken with him. He is a man I have admired for a great many years, and I was literally trembling–no exaggeration–trembling just to be in his presence.

But what struck me was that he had both a set of facts and a well-documented story. The facts include his horrendous stay in a Nazi concentration camp and the loss of home and family during the Holocaust. That he suffered beyond both description and imagination is a fact. Nothing can change that fact. But the story, the story of his life is that he survived, that he has told the story for those who could not tell the story themselves, that he has worked tirelessly for human rights around the world, that he still, in spite of the facts, loves life and food and friends, and that he still loves God, even though part of his story has been an ongoing quarrel with God. That's his story. You can't change the facts. That's history. You can choose the story. That's hope.

I think a lot of us have it all wrong. So many times we want God to come down to Earth and rearrange the facts of our lives. To hear some Christians talk, God is upstairs rearranging the furniture on Earth all the time. Yet I'm not sure God is in the business of rearranging our facts. But if the Christian faith has any vitality, if it is fundamentally true in any kind of coherent way, then God is in the business of changing our stories. Your story and my story. Changing it one person at a time. One story at a time. One attitude at a time. God helps me understand that my life in this world is not located merely in the facts of my life but in the story of my life, and that's where I have the power to choose to live with hope.

Jesus was born, and suddenly there was an energy of God released into the world; creative, transforming, loving energy exploded in the world. On the one hand, the facts of the world haven't changed all that much since his birth. We still have violence. We still have our politics and politicians. Families still struggle to stay together. People still get sick and people still die. In one way of looking at it, since the birth of Jesus there has been nothing new under the sun. But in another way of thinking about it, everything has changed since that first Christmas because we now know that God is forever transforming the world by forever transforming us, by loving us, by promising never to abandon us, inspiring us with the necessary courage to face even the most dreadful of facts. It's in our story that we decide to live with courage. Or we decide to live with gratitude. Or we decide to live with openness and kindness and joy; yes, even joy is a choice we make.

Several years ago I found a quote from the philosopher Teilhard de Chardin that continues to define for me the essence of faith. The words were found scribbled on a piece of paper on his desk after his death. Sometimes all the soul needs is a scribbled note. In a flash of brilliance he wrote, "A presence is never mute." Not a bad scrap to live by. "A presence is never mute." Though sometimes we think it is. Sometimes we feel it is. Sometimes other people try to convince us that it is. "A presence is never mute." Arising from the ruins of our living is a stubborn, faithful, gracious presence, and this presence, this presence of God, offers healing to us again and again.

The best I can determine, there are two places where Christians locate God's hope. There are some Christians who locate hope in some great future event that God will accomplish. The second coming of Jesus. The establishment of the kingdom of God upon the earth. Some great apocalyptic firestorm and the creation of a new heaven and a new earth. There is a wide segment of our culture that has literalized such an end to the world. Personally, I think such end-time scenarios are misguided and fundamentally betray the hopefulness of God. Fred Craddock has playfully posed the idea that the reason why some Christians are so focused on the second coming of Jesus is because they are secretly disappointed in the first coming of Jesus. From my perspective, it's not what God *will* do that is the basis of hope; it's what God *is* doing that gives rise to hope and, even more radically, what God is always wanting to do. I don't know what God will do tomorrow, but I know that today God is calling me to open my heart, live life with integrity, move toward my neighbor with compassion and justice, heal the most important relationships within the web of my life. The whole point of the spiritual journey is that God calls people to move forward with trust and courage into the future because God is taking the raw stuff of everyday living and trying to turn it, shape it, create from it something beautiful and good.

Hope is the daily excavation work of God, and excavation surely has to begin with *courage*. Courage literally means *heart*. It is the capacity to feel. It is the capacity to experience. There is no spirituality without the exercise of personal courage because it always takes courage to open the heart. And that of course is where healing begins; it begins in the depths of the heart. Healing of a specific childhood wound, for example, can never happen without finding courage to open the heart. There might be a devastating betrayal in our history, and healing can happen from that betrayal, but not without first finding the courage to live with it for a while. We all make mistakes, some of them quite costly in terms of emotional damage to ourselves and others, but healing can happen, and it happens when we find the courage to face up to our responsibilities. Feeling what the heart needs to feel is often the first step toward healing a relationship. The courageous heart believes that the ache of hope outweighs the pain of the past.

I also think about the essential nature of *forgiveness* in the experience of healing. At some point, all of us arrive at a place where the only alternative in a relationship is forgiveness. The clock cannot be turned back. The script cannot be rewritten. The facts cannot be improved. At such moments the circle is only completed by way of forgiveness. The choice of forgiveness is profound. The alternative is bitterness, anger, and irreparable damage to our own souls. Forgiveness is essential, not so much for the other person, but for ourselves. Not as an act of selfishness, but surely an act of well-being for all concerned. We do our souls a favor when we forgive. And yes, sometimes we must learn the art of forgiving ourselves. Frederick Buechner describes forgiveness in this way: "For both parties, forgiveness means the freedom again to be at peace inside their own skins and to be glad in each other's presence."[3] In many ways, forgiveness is more about the future than it is the past. Traditionally, forgiveness has been associated with the forgiving of some past sin. However, understood a little differently, forgiveness is the granting of permission to live life right now, moving into the future with zest and vitality.

Related to the soul's healing is the gift of *imagination*. Imagination is simply looking at the world in a fresh way, reshaping a perspective, providing a different frame for the reality that stubbornly is. Imagination suggests that all reality is ultimately inward. People who have suffered horribly can still maintain their dignity because the defining reality is on the inside of their souls. By the way, Jesus gave this gift to people again and again. He did not give them a different world; he gave them a different way of looking at the world. To imagine the past differently enables us to reclaim it with renewed meaning and purpose. And almost always, when imagination is engaged and allowed to flourish, then compassion follows. It requires so little imagination to remain a victim, but to survive, to thrive, to experience healing and hope requires a new set of eyes.

Taken together, these realities constitute the essence of hope that is the essence of God. The human spirit thrives in the presence of hope. Hope is confident expectation, not that everything will turn out as we like, but that no matter how things turn out, we know and feel ourselves held in the arms of love. That is to say, a presence abides. Hope is the porch light that shines through the night welcoming us home and reminding us that we have a place in the world. It's the one phone call that comes when everyone else has stopped calling. It's the card that comes from an old friend that simply says, "You are loved." The circle of life remains unbroken as long as there is a presence of hope. What it means for a human heart to lose hope is incalculable. But the presence of hope takes even the most tragic losses, turning them over again and again and again, the way a plow cuts the earth, promising the possibility that some new thing, some new moment will grow from this life. Our personal histories surge and crest like great waves, but God offers a possibility for each occasion of our experience; indeed, God's gift to the world is the future, born moment by moment and available in the living now of our lives.

The soul longs for healing, both to receive it and to give it. That brokenness is part of the universe is clearly seen each and every day. But brokenness is not the only word. Living alongside us and within us is an invitation from the universe, the very invitation offered by Jesus to the people of his day and the invitation heard long ago by Abraham and Sarah. It is the opportunity to open the heart, to be loved and accepted, to be held in the arms of something great and wonderful as we journey forth. The universe is alive with such healing. In the silence of even our darkest hours there are waves rising and falling in the ceaseless rhythms of human experience. Rising and falling. Rising and falling. Wave after wave washing over us, washing through us, waves of love, of grace, waves of the divine that heal the human soul.

CHAPTER EIGHT

Respecting the Many Paths

*Home is the ground of our being where God's love
encompasses and envelops us; little by little, it opens us to
recognize our unity with all that is. We belong in unity. We
are made for truth and love; truth and love mean oneness
with each other and with God.*

ELAINE PREVELLET[1]

I could tell by the intensity of his voice that I was in for a
roller coaster of a conversation. I was at a party. Lots of people.
Loud music. Good food. I was standing out by the pool in one
of those in-between party creases. Having just finished up one
conversation, I found myself standing alone for a few minutes
enjoying an iced tea and trying to eat a few bites of spicy Texas
barbeque.

Brian came up to me with an urgent look, not panicky, but
clearly more than ready for a specific conversation. Even though
he looked vaguely familiar to me, I didn't know him. Evidently
he knew me, because the first question out of his mouth was
"Aren't you that minister over at University Christian Church?"

"Hmm," I thought to myself, "*that* minister."

Although I was tempted to plead not guilty, I decided it was best to come clean and ride the roller coaster of this encounter. The poet Rainer Maria Rilke once encouraged a young man to learn to love the questions. I continue to be amazed at how important that is, not only to love my own questions—and I have plenty of them—but to love the questions of others. One of the most spiritually affirming gestures we can make toward another human being is to give the gift of our listening, listening to the questions that swirl inside the heart, sometimes like a gentle breeze, sometimes like a great storm, listening to the deepest questions of the human spirit. To question is to be alive. To listen to questions is to share aliveness with others.

He started to explain, "Well, I'm not a member of your church, but I have a lot of friends who are, and I've heard some of them say that you believe people of other religions are going to go to heaven, and that it doesn't really matter what you believe, and I guess what I wanted to know is if you really believe that, and if so, how can you believe that when the Bible is so clear that Jesus is the only way to God? I mean, I go to church every Sunday, but if it doesn't matter what you really believe, then why am I even wasting my time?"

A little part of me secretly thought, "Why can't I just talk about the weather like everybody else?"

Maybe there was a tinge of accusation in Brian's questions, I don't know, but he seemed sincere to me, someone genuinely trying to make sense of his faith. Like a lot of people who go to church Sunday after Sunday, he had gotten caught on the jagged splinters of his own theology. On the one hand, he was trying to be true to a particular theological outlook he assumed was biblical, a religious system he considered to be the Truth with a capital *T* for all time. On the other hand, I also suspect he was feeling uneasy with this viewpoint, wondering, for example, how Christians can be the only people in the world God loves, wondering how God could reject Jewish people in favor of Christian people, wondering how a God of love could actually condemn the majority of the world's population to some form of everlasting hell, wondering if the Bible has to be interpreted so literally, wondering how he could make sense of his view of God in light of his friendships with people who were not Christians.

Brian was searching. He had the right passion and sincerity and seriousness about his relationship with God, but what he needed was at least another alternative way of looking at faith. He needed a theological perspective big enough for his sincerity or maybe some different ideas that could enhance his identity as a Christian while at the same time opening up an authentic dialogue with other people. Maybe he needed some ideas that could become lenses through which he could look at himself and the world, and ultimately some ideas that could help him see a different kind of God. No one has all the right ideas. But there are some ideas better than others, just as there are some ideas more intellectually and spiritually coherent than others, and some ideas more morally appropriate than others, and some ideas that make more sense than others. Ideas make certain claims about how we see ourselves and others and God and, even more to the point, how we treat ourselves and others and God. Religion is deeply personal. That can never be denied. At the same time, I'm not sure it's helpful to reduce religion to a mere "this is what I feel" kind of approach. Religion, just as other areas of our lives, needs to hang together in some credible way.

Brian's outlook on faith was extremely literal. He wanted to hold on to his Christian faith, to be sure, and I wanted that for him too, but Christian faith should open doors, not close them. Make the world larger, not smaller. It's a faith that I continue to call *ecumenical,* an *ecu-faith,* and it's a faith characterized by openness to understanding Christian identity, not defined over against other people in the world, but a faith that is all-embracing toward the human family.

What's interesting to me is that virtually every person Jesus touched became more engaged in a larger world. Jesus was the great perspective-giver, helping people see themselves and others differently. Helping people imagine life differently. I think of the gospel story of the man healed of leprosy. Suddenly his world became bigger because of the touch of Jesus. The blind man touched by Jesus sees the whole world in a new way. The story of the good Samaritan was really a world-breaking, eye-opening, mind-clearing parable about seeing and thinking of the world differently. Ecu-faith is a celebration of Jesus Christ and a generous dance outwardly to those who are different.

It's too easy for many of us to hold a faith that has become like a cotton sweater shrunk in the dryer. Too small. Too tight. Too confining. Brian was serious about his faith, and such seriousness should not be underestimated, but what I think he needed was the light touch of grace and mystery and surprise. A less predictable, less regimented faith. A faith that was more poetry than explanation. But what I also realized, standing there by the pool trying to have a bite of dinner, was that there was something I could learn from him. That's the true give-and-take of the faith experience. His dark, swirling, Van Gogh-like questions were not his alone. I have mine as well. As does every Christian courageous enough to think them and feel them and ask them.

It probably can't be said enough, true spirituality emerges from our questions. It's important to pay attention to our questions, even those questions that might change the way we think and feel and believe. It's part of opening the heart. Sometimes my questions are intellectual in nature. True faith is never threatened by true intellectual questions. The very act of asking, exploring, and searching is part of the spiritual pilgrimage the soul wants to take. In this way, our curiosities and intuitions about faith often become important keys to unlocking a deeper understanding of life. Even in reading the sacred stories of the Bible, the most important posture is not correct interpretation, but listening for insight that surprises and delights and, yes, even puzzles.

Questions: How can I believe in my particular faith while at the same time respecting people of different faiths? If I'm a Christian, how can I believe that Jesus is Lord and Savior, the very words I confessed before the church at my baptism when I was twelve years old, and avoid being arrogant, exclusive, judgmental toward people of the Jewish faith, Islamic faith, Buddhist faith? What can I do with those passages in the Bible that seem to imply Jesus is the only way to God, not just one way but the only way? What can I do with those parts of the

Christian tradition that condemn people of the Jewish faith? Is there a way for me to be a Christian while accepting from, even learning from, people of different faiths, recognizing that there is something profound all people of every faith ultimately share on the spiritual journey? Should I try to convert people to the Christian faith?

How we answer these kinds of questions is important, because in the end they are questions about what kind of human beings we will be in this world. More than anything, spirituality should enhance our humanity. It has always been strange to me how some people who seemingly become more and more explicit in their Christian language and practice–going to Bible studies, getting active in their churches, and so on–actually become less and less enjoyable as human beings. In the words of Mark Twain, "Some people become so heavenly minded that they are no earthly good at all!" The very appeal of Jesus was that he lived his life with an evocative sense of humanity. He became transparent, if you will, a window into the very soul of God. It was not the divinity of Jesus that revealed God to the world, it was his humanity, full, rich, and textured, that helped people see the true essence of the divine reality.

Even a cursory look at the history of civilization reveals that religion has often done the very opposite. Inhumane treatment of others in the name of religion has left a bloody stain upon everyone who claims to be a Christian. Anti-Judaism. Violent crusades. Degradation of women. Systemic racism toward African Americans. Persecution of gay and lesbian persons. Disrespect toward older adults. Frankly, I don't blame anyone who is suspicious of any kind of religious faith, given the atrocities perpetrated upon the world in the name of God. Brian's questions were good questions. They opened up a dimension of spirituality, not just the inward journey of his own feelings toward God, but the outward journey in terms of how people should be treated. Real faith is ultimately expressed in how we treat others.

Like most people, I arrived at graduate school with all the answers and, in the end, I left with a bulging suitcase full of questions. Part of what happened to me during that time, and what is now woven into the very fabric of my own faith experience, was a deeper and deeper appreciation for the questions of faith. The heart opens itself to the great "Other" of the universe by opening itself to the deepest questions of existence. Sometimes the questions shook the very foundation of my existence. At other times, the questions were exciting, moments of true liberation. But it's also true that the heart cannot merely be open to the questions of faith; it has to be open to other people, other men and women who are also asking their questions and seeking their answers.

It was fascinating watching the world ring in a new millennium. Time zone by time zone by time zone, celebration gradually moved around the planet until all of us were in the year 2000 together. What was so vivid to me as I watched the live millennial coverage was the compelling truth that we may be in different time zones and have different languages and enjoy different customs, but we are all part of the same planet. And in spite of language differences and skin color differences and faith differences, we are truly part of the same human family. This energy we call God mysteriously moves through the lives of others, lives, inspires, touches the world through other men and women. Therefore, the heart can never be fully open until the genuine experiences of others, their thoughts, their ideas, their beliefs, are taken into our own experience. One way to think about spirituality is that it is the vocational call of listening to our deepest voice. But spirituality is also the process of listening to the grand chorus of voices surrounding our lives and filling our world each day. These are the voices of the human family. Our sisters. Our brothers.

I remember in graduate school being exposed to people of different faiths and theologies, different backgrounds and cultures. But these viewpoints were not merely intellectual differences. These were real people, people with very human qualities and aspirations, people I had grown to enjoy before and after classes, and yet, often, we held very different commitments toward faith. They were all exceptionally bright. And as far as I could tell, they were all sincere. It didn't take long for me to realize that religion was not about being smart enough. Not about getting all the answers right. That doesn't mean people should give up on the idea that faith should be in the business of seeking understanding, it's just that the driving force of faith really can't be figuring it all out in order to have all the pieces of the cosmic puzzle in their right places.

I began to realize in that graduate school environment that religion has very little to do with being right, though that's exactly what Brian was fishing for at that party long ago. He wanted to know if *my* faith or *his* faith was right. There's a phrase from the Jewish scriptures that reads, "No one has ever seen the face of God." That's more than poetic phrasing. It's a deep commentary on the essence of faith. The faith experience is not about being smart enough. It's not about getting it all right, theologically, morally, ethically, philosophically. What an oppressive venture that would be anyway! The faith experience is about finding a certain sense of resonance, of meaning, of vibrato in daily life with the presence of the holy. There's a reason why religion inspires artists and poets and musicians, because, in the end, they are all trying to describe that which defies description. In the final analysis, aren't we all called to be mystics?

I remember getting to know a professor who was Jewish. I realized after listening to his lecture week after week that he didn't necessarily *become* Jewish, at least not in the sense of a conversion to Judaism. Born in New York City to Jewish parents, he was Jewish by birth, not choice. Additionally, he was male by birth. Even as he was American by birth. Even as he was upper middle-class by birth. No real choice in his situation, just statistical freakishness. And the same could be said for the woman professor visiting from Japan. She was Buddhist. She never became a Buddhist, as if it were a completely conscious choice on her part. She was just Buddhist.

Well, if he was Jewish because he was Jewish, and she was Buddhist because she was Buddhist, then in my case I had to admit that I was really a Christian because, well, because I was Christian, not to mention American, not to mention male, not to mention white, not to mention middle-class. What a humbling moment it was to recognize that I was Christian because I happened to be born to two parents who also happened to be Christians, who happened to be members of First Christian Church, which happened to be located at

201 E. Walnut Street in Salem, Indiana, which happened to carry within it certain values and beliefs and faith stories that I had assumed most of my life, at least up until entering graduate school, were unquestionably right. I realized, and not without some anguish, that the structure of my faith wasn't necessarily right nor was it necessarily wrong. I realized that my faith was part of a non-chosen cultural system.

What a turning point! I am who I am, and you are who you are, partly by choice, but partly because of a freakish, capricious, unpredictable convergence of life events. That very idea started blowing through my little faith like a tornado in Kansas moving across a field of wheat, and for a while, more than humbling to my faith system, it felt destructive and dangerous to my faith system. But fact is fact. A spirituality that doesn't take truth seriously is no spirituality at all. Years removed from those graduate school realizations, I now see it was no tornado blowing through my faith, but it was the fresh air, fresh breath, fresh wind of God blowing through my too-narrow little world. It was time for me to enlarge my faith. Time to move from a religion of rightness to an ecu-way of living inspired by the gospel.

After all, how could God let all these people be born Buddhist? Born Buddhist just to live and die and go to hell? That's ludicrous! What kind of God is that? What kind of universe is that? How could God, the very God about whom I had been taught in Sunday school and vacation Bible school, the God who was both great and good, how could God let a little child be born Jewish or Islamic or Hindu? That would be nothing less than an act of divine cruelty if indeed the only way to God is the Christian way to God. Where did I get this only one way, right way, my way or no way kind of theology? It wasn't making sense to me theologically anymore. It wasn't making sense intellectually anymore. And in light of my friendships with people of different faiths, it wasn't making sense experientially anymore. What started out as a graduate school problem became much more serious; it became a spiritual crisis, the very experience genuine faith is trying to create.

Some of you might even laugh at such questions today— I'm tempted to look back and laugh as well—but all I can say is that it was no laughing matter to me as my faith opened and stretched, attempting to give birth to a wriggling, messy, wondrous new way of thinking and feeling about God. Therefore, as tempting as it is for me to laugh, I know it would betray the true core of my spiritual experience. But I can't really laugh for another reason. I think about my conversation with Brian that night at the party. And not just Brian, but many people both inside and outside the church community. Brian was trying to make sense of a small faith in a big world, and that's always a momentous occasion.

Part of my larger hope for the church is that Christians can find a way to define their faith and build their identity without its being cast in the black and white dichotomy that "We're right and you're wrong." I'm passionate about my Christian faith. I love Jesus Christ with my entire being. But the very essence of Jesus Christ reminds me that the spiritual search transcends any particular culture or pathway or belief system. Furthermore, God is not cruel, nor is God capricious. If people are created in the image of God, then all people, regardless of their pathway, are fundamentally connected to God. I think Christians have something to say to people of other faiths, and people of other faiths have something to say to us. There is an authentic way of confessing faith in Christ while at the same time being respectful of others. That's what I tried to communicate to Brian that night. No laughing matter to be sure, but a conversation that stretched us both.

CHAPTER NINE

The Human Touch

*Every human sucks the living strength of God from a
different place, said Rabbi Pinhas, and together they make
up Man. Perhaps as humans deepen and widen their
understanding of God, it takes more people to see the whole
of him. Or it could be that there is a universal mind for
whom we are all strangers.*

ANNIE DILLARD[1]

It seems like such a modest thing to suggest religious faith
should actually humanize the world. Unfortunately, this has
not always been the case. By humanize I mean that experience
of creating a greater capacity for relationships among people.
Relationships of depth and mystery. Shared feeling. Common
respect. By humanize I also mean creating greater appreciation
for human vulnerability. More acceptance toward human
diversity. More compassion toward human failure. The
humanizing factor of faith extends outward toward others, but
it also reaches inward, allowing people that magical experience

of listening to their own lives in gracious and forgiving ways. This is part of what I would call the larger hope for the church.

To humanize the world is not the same as humanism. Humanism is an ideology claiming the only reality in the world is human reality. No mystery. No wonder. What you see is what you get. What I'm suggesting is not at all like humanism. In fact, just the opposite. A true turning point of faith is the realization that there is indeed more to life than meets the eye. There is depth, and divine reality within that depth. There is God, but not the God "up there" somewhere, "out there" somewhere, but the God woven into the very fabric of each day. The reality of God is the ground of all human experience, the infrastructure of all thinking and feeling and being in the world. This is the God beyond God, the God that is deeper than even theism.

Drive through New York City or Washington, D.C., during the winter, and what you will see is steam coming up through the manhole covers. The rising steam is a reminder that there is a whole world underneath the surface of the city. This is how I understand human experience. God is the underground energy, the soul-steam that turns and drives and empowers all living. As I understand it, and admittedly all understanding of God consists of bits and pieces and fragments, this divine reality is both beyond and within human experience. Therefore, to touch divine reality means we have to open up and touch our humanity and the humanity of others. It's in the human touch that we find the divine spirit.

Our humanity is both a gift from God and a call from God. I'm afraid many expressions of the Christian faith encourage people in one way or another to move away from their humanity. Viewed from a certain perspective, I can appreciate this emphasis. After all, life should not consist of doing whatever we "damn well please" and acting on every impulse that happens to run through our reptilian brains. On the other hand, life is not about denying our humanity, as if the "flesh" were evil. Nor is it about loathing our humanity, though guilt and shame seem to be religious staples in most churches. And maybe I should also add that it's not about constantly trying to improve our humanity, in spite of the fact that most preaching tends to be moralistic. Life is a gift God calls us to live, recognizing that the process of growing into our own soulful skin is the most sacred process of our existence.

Here's what I remember about seeing my mother a few weeks before her death. I remember the last day of January in the year 2000 was a snowy day in Indianapolis. I remember having a conversation with my mother. Maybe the most significant conversation she and I ever had. She had recently been diagnosed with cancer, and I had gone back home to Indianapolis to visit her. I was acutely aware that in all probability it would be my last visit with her. It was.

She and I sat on the sofa for a few hours that morning. She told me how she was feeling. She was so clear as she spoke to me that day. She talked about how she was trying to live one day at a time. How she was grateful for each moment of life. How she was now storing up cherished memories, refusing to fall into the trap of feeling sorry for herself. Nor did she want others to feel sorry for her. She was aware that life was about to drain from her body over the upcoming weeks; at the same time, she was spiritually full and vital.

She spoke of our old house, a large three-story home on Main Street—stifling hot in the summer and cold and drafty in the winter—but a magnificent house nevertheless. Even now, the more I remember that old house, the more I love it. She mentioned memories of cookouts and holiday dinners, how my friends would always fill up the house when I was in high school. I started to remember all the good times there. Pitch and catch with my dad in the backyard. Basketball games. The drudgery of mowing the yard. I also know we had some not-so-good times there. That's true of most houses. I can't deny the painful times. The ambiguous times. It's just that as the snow continued falling on that January day, huge, heavy, wet snowflakes falling to the ground, I was reminded that there really is such a thing as grace in life. Grace in just being in the presence of another human being.

As my mother was talking, it struck me that the real secret to life is to get to the place where our bodies are ready to empty into the earth like rivers of sand emptying into the desert while at the same time our soul, or that essence of depth within each of us, is brimming over with the treasure of human experience, full of memories, full of joy, full of meaning. Jesus urged his disciples to "store up treasures in heaven." But where is heaven? Surely it is the human heart. Or God's heart. Or both. Such treasuring, however, is not easy for most of us. Our lives are riddled with ambiguity and anxiety, painful experiences so hard, if not impossible, to release.

My mother told me that she was loving being surrounded by compassionate friends and family, so grateful to the people who were caring for her, especially my sister who had come to mean so much to her over the past years. She even told me that she was sorry for mistakes she had made as a mother. That was like drilling into the nerve of one of my teeth. Yes, she had made some mistakes, and those mistakes had created hurt between the two of us. I grew up missing, not all the time, but sometimes missing her tenderness and gentleness and softness. Qualities she sometimes had a difficult time expressing. But I had made mistakes too. It's strange how you get to a place in life where the mistakes really don't matter. Maybe they shouldn't matter so much in the first place. As she talked to me that day I could feel emotion crawling up my throat like a cat. Through the years I had accumulated distance with my mother like frequent flyer miles. So much felt. So little said. And then she said it, she flat out said it. She uttered the words as matter-of-factly as they could be said. She told me she loved me, that she was proud of me, told me how much I had meant to her. Unlike the snow outside on the ground, I melted.

That winter day in Indianapolis was one of the most human moments of my life. Everything was pure and clear and simple. It was a moment of depth. It was real. It was meaningful. It was also a moment when I felt a presence both within me and moving between us, a presence I call God. What's so amazing as I think back on that morning is that I was reminded of how wonderful it is to see another person's humanity, to see them from a slightly different angle. That's not easy for a son or daughter to do. I began to see her as a human being far more courageous and thoughtful than I ever thought possible. Here was someone who could look at the ending of her life and be grateful for the experiences that had constituted her living. I couldn't help but think that day about all the other people in my life I have failed to see, failed to see the gift of their God-infused humanity, their brokenness and beauty, and best of all, the beauty within their brokenness.

Metaphors matter. They not only reflect what we believe about God, but they can also inspire new ways of thinking, feeling, believing. That's exactly what was whispering through my brain as I talked to Brian that night at the party or as I thought about Suzanne sitting in church Sunday after Sunday. These were two human beings in need of new metaphors, new images for what it means to have faith in God. I found a metaphor in my conversation with my mother. A metaphor that unlocks some of God's essence. My mother had indeed loved me with all her flawed humanity, and I had received that love with all my flawed humanity, but without a doubt, love was present. No matter how poorly expressed. No matter how inadequately understood. Love was present.

This is why I suggested to Brian at one point in our conversation that there's nothing in the world stronger than a mother's love. At times gentle. At times fierce. And always, always active, engaged, participatory in the lives of children. I think of how my mother loved not only me, but also my sister Nancy and my brother John. All three of us were—and are—very different from one another. But she loved each of us uniquely. I see my wife, Marti, love our three children. Again, all three of them are very different in personality and interest. Yet she loves them, not in some blanket way, but she loves each of them uniquely. She takes into account Matthew's argumentative intellect and Drew's quiet introversion and Katie's exuberant extroversion. She is mother to them all, of course, but the love she exercises is complex and multi-dimensional. It would be too simplistic for her to treat all three of them the same. She doesn't. She knows how to give each of them the love they individually need. There is a big difference in loving someone the way we want to love them and loving someone the way they need to be loved.

What I have come to appreciate more and more about God, and what I offered to Brian that night, is that God loves people with complex precision. God is not simplistic. God is not without nuance. God loves the world uniquely, in tailor-made fashion, loves the world not only for what it should be, but for what it is in all its multicolored, multicultural, multireligious ways. If anyone can recognize the different paths people travel on the spiritual journey and appreciate those different paths for all their unique beauty, it is God. If anyone can appreciate human uniqueness, it is God. If anyone can enjoy diversity in the human experience, it is God. No wonder there are so many different religions in the world, and even more individualized spiritualities; it's because people are complex. But like a mother who skillfully takes each child into account, passionately wrapping her life around them in unique fashion, so also God loves the human family.

To me, this makes divine love truly awesome and full of wonder. The importance of wonder is everything! And to follow the metaphor even further, God looks upon Christians and loves Christians uniquely, appreciating all the strength and value released into the world through Christians. There is validity in the Christian faith. As a Christian I believe that divine love and creativity were released into the world through Jesus of Nazareth and that this invitation to receive divine love is made known to the world through Christian community, the followers of Jesus we call the church. Through rituals like communion and baptism, through preaching and deeds of service, through witness and advocacy in the world, the church becomes transparent so that people are able to see the living presence of Jesus. And though I can appreciate other faiths, I have no intention of being anything other than a Christian. I will be baptized until my death and nothing will ever change that.

Nevertheless, just because I believe the Christian faith has validity and authenticity, that doesn't mean I have to believe that it *alone* has validity. If I've come to know divine love through the Christian faith, that love should then open my heart wider and wider and wider toward the experiences of others. The world is humanized one heart at a time. And just as the Golden Gate Bridge stretches out across the bay from San Francisco to Sausalito, so also the human heart stretches, opens, reaches beyond itself to the hearts of others. It makes sense to me, therefore, that God also looks upon the person of Buddhist faith, appreciating the depth of faith and truth and authenticity that exists in that particular religious expression. And God looks upon the Jewish person, uniquely loving the Jewish man or woman because of the rich heritage of the Jewish scriptures and Torah and stories. And God looks upon the Muslim in the same way. And God looks upon the Protestant or Catholic in the same way. To appreciate this encompassing divine presence doesn't mean that all religions are the same—they are not—but it does suggest that at a fundamental level they are all reaching toward both the unreachable and unknowable quality of God.

Denise Levertov has a short poem that reads:

Scraps of moon
bobbing discarded on broken water
but sky-moon
complete, transcending
all violation.[2]

I am moved by this poem because it reminds me that there is a difference between the wholeness we want and the partialness we must learn to live with. Just as God is one, so also in the eyes of God, the human family is one. To appreciate this oneness of humanity is of utmost importance, and surely it is a foundational dimension of faith. More than that, it is a theological commitment toward life. We do have a partialness—the fragmented moon bobbing upon the water—but to embrace the fragmentation is an act of faith. The apostle Paul put it like this: "We look into a mirror, dimly." I think it's important that Christians recognize the partialness of faith. I also think it's important that Christians never add to the already fragmentary nature of the world. Ecu-faith seeks to nurture the wholeness that is implicitly there.

What I proposed to Brian that night is that Christians have often been the ones who have built walls, waged holy wars, decided who was religiously "in" and religiously "out." But that isn't really our job. Jesus himself said, "Judge not lest you be judged." God is the one who loves inclusively and uniquely. The fact that God can love in such a multidimensional way doesn't water down the Christian faith, nor any faith; if anything, it makes the love of God more appealing and inviting.

Therefore, what I try to appreciate is that there are many different paths to the divine, and what is called for on my part is respect and love for my fellow travelers. As we're learning all too well, especially after our national disaster of September 11, 2001, the world will never come to find the peace and harmony it deserves until people of different faiths and cultures learn how to talk to and appreciate one another. How can Christians do anything less than embrace the human spirit that thrives within all kinds of people, in all kinds of places, guided by all kinds of faith?

There's an interesting Jesus story found in the gospel of Luke that sheds light on this radically inclusive understanding of God. There was a man who was not walking the Jewish path but who had become a dear friend of the Jewish community. He helped build their synagogue. He supported their efforts as a community. He also became very interested in Jesus, wanting Jesus to heal one of his servants, who was near death. Jesus responds to the man. Respects the man. Jesus says to this man on a different path, "I tell you, not even among those walking the Jewish path have I seen such incredible, such vibrant, such dynamic faith." That is not condemnation toward Jews; it is profound respect for someone walking a different religious path.

If Jesus could respect those walking different paths, if Jesus could see that giving respect in no way diminished his own path, if Jesus could be open to dialogue with someone not on his personal path, then doesn't it make sense that Christians exhibit the same openness to others? I mean, shouldn't followers of Jesus, shouldn't they, shouldn't *we,* show respect, be open to learn, be open to share, be willing to travel alongside those who, for whatever reason, might be on a different path? And if we do that, doesn't that mean the church is making a safer world, a more whole and sane world, and doesn't that mean the church is acting toward others the way Jesus acted? Don't you think a little more respect in the world would be a good thing? I mean, after yet another school shooting, after more ethnic cleansing, after more human rights violations, don't you think the world could use all the respect and dignity the church can give it?

And then, of course, I think of the world before and after our new day of infamy, September 11, 2001. On that Tuesday morning America watched with horror as commercial airliners crashed into the World Trade Towers, the Pentagon, the Pennsylvania countryside. There are so many lessons to be learned from this great American wound, but surely one of them is the realization of how utterly dangerous religious and political fanaticism is to the human family. Those hijackers no more represented the genuine faith of Islam than Timothy McVeigh represented Christianity. Fanaticism is dangerous, but not because people hold passionately their faith. There's nothing wrong with that. Indeed, I wish more people were passionate about their faith. The problem with fanaticism is that it is religious rightness to the exclusion of others. Moreover, it's not that other people are viewed as wrong, but that other people are seen as the enemy, and for the life of me, I don't know why a religion needs an enemy to have a reason for being. Whether it is Islamic extremism or Christian fundamentalism, it makes the world a dangerous place to live.

I am a Christian walking the Christian path; Jesus Christ is my way to God; I confess him as Lord and Savior to the glory of God; and I will arrive at God the Father/Mother/Friend through him. For me it will only be through him. That's why my Christian faith means everything to me. I am passionate about it. But isn't there a way to love the path we are on while respecting those who are walking different paths? Perhaps if we would avail ourselves of more human moments—true human experiences of knowing others, learning of their struggles and joys—perhaps then we would begin to discover God in a more substantive way. Perhaps we would learn in the midst of genuine human encounter that God is big enough for all of us. And maybe, just maybe, we will get to the place where we can believe in a God that is at least as big as the one Jesus believed in.

CHAPTER TEN

The Great Mountain of God

Every moment and every event of every man's life on earth plants something in his soul...In all situations of life the will of God comes to us not merely as an external dictate of impersonal law but above all as an interior motivation of personal love.

THOMAS MERTON[1]

The heart opens wider and wider, welcoming home the stranger that is within us, but also taking unto itself the fellow pilgrim, other human beings whom we meet along the way. Maybe it's a friend or a member of our own family. Perhaps it's someone we meet briefly in a business setting. Or maybe it's the person who is completely different from us—different gender, different religion, different race—but somehow we feel the hinges of our hearts loosen a bit, and we welcome into our very selves the life of another person. To experience grace is to experience the heart of God, but to allow grace to become graciousness is to carry God to the world.

In a little letter found in the New Testament, the book of First John, the writer suggests, "Whoever loves a brother or a sister lives in the light." In another place the same writer offers, "Let us love one another because love is from God." And still again, "If we love one another, God lives within us."

These words of wisdom are reminders that within the act of opening our hearts toward other people, there is something deep and profound that flows back to us. It is more than a feeling. More than a psychological response. It is nothing less than the presence of God; Spirituality is more than having a privatized feeling about God, it is also about being connected to one another in a profoundly human way. To walk the Christian path means we are in darkness until we can see the light of God in the faces of others, some walking the same path, some walking different paths. Where is God? God is as close to us as the next loving gesture or the forthcoming kind word to another human being. God is in the eyes, in the heart, in the life of the person sitting next to us at any given moment in life.

I'm not exactly sure when it happened, but from those adolescent years of a black-and-white faith, my experience broadened to become more open to people who were walking different journeys. I started to attach my heart to their hearts. Not just their beliefs or religious traditions, but the entire experience of their believing. Faith had a face, and in the faces of others I started seeing the rightness of their faith. Not rightness in the sense that someone is right and someone is wrong, but rightness that is authenticity and truthfulness, rightness that is emotional, psychological, and spiritual reality. These people were not the enemies. The enemies are not, nor should they ever have been, the Catholics or Protestants or Jews or Muslims or Buddhists. If there is any enemy at all, it is the enemy deep within our own psyches, that enemy called self-hatred and human insecurity. The enemy called fear. It is the enemy called prejudice, self-righteousness, and arrogance.

An open, searching, ecumenical faith started to grow from my questions, and my sense is that Christians of all denominations are also searching to have an inclusive faith that embraces the diversity of the human family. How could I condemn someone of a different faith? How could I paint myself into such a small God-corner when God is not small at all? When the world is so enormous in scope, fabulous in complexity, beautiful in diversity, how could I think that some have God and some don't? How could I judge others given the radiance of the human faces behind the different religions of the world? What I had to face, and continue to face, in my own faith was a kind of religious, cultural, and spiritual arrogance. It was naive to be sure, and as far as I know it was never malicious, but it was arrogant nevertheless. What I passionately care about now is finding a spirituality that enhances the humanity of all people and, in turn, the church making a contribution to a safer, more whole, more sane world. Surely the world should expect that of the church.

Beyond any kind of flaccid tolerance of a "live and let live" kind of attitude, I started to listen to others and learn from others, and continue to do so to this day. It is part of my faith experience. People of various faiths are no longer threats to be avoided nor objects to be converted. They are people who can enhance my faith experience. And maybe I can enhance their experience, too. I long for the dialogue. Relish the sharing. Love the common respect. And especially I appreciate the common humanity that exists among people of faith, regardless of their particular cultural or religious expression. Different concepts of faith can be seen as complementary and not competing. There are stories and myths that are shared, concepts that approximate one another, beliefs that clearly grow from the banks of the same river. Yes, what I now see again and again is that there is a powerful river of energy that runs underneath everyone courageous enough to open his or her heart to the universe, to the great, wild energy of God that pulses in all things.

I'm reminded of the time I had a chance to hear the Dalai Lama speak in Louisville, Kentucky. He looked both beautiful and serene in his gold and red robes. But what I remember most about that encounter is that it did not matter that day if we were Christian or Buddhist or Jew or Muslim. It just didn't matter. For in a childlike way, which is another way of saying, a Christlike way, the Dalai Lama opened his address by saying,

"Today I meet you as human beings." It's always beautiful when people meet as human beings, beautiful and profoundly spiritual. God is so intertwined in our humanity that it's hard to separate our humanity and God's divinity. It's like moving a plant from one pot to a bigger pot; when you finally pull it out, what you see are tangled, weblike roots, so matted together that it's hard to know where one root begins and another ends. The human spirit and God's spirit are tangled beautifully.

There's another metaphor that makes sense to me as I piece together my faith. I continue to use the metaphor of path and journey and pilgrimage to describe the faith experience. Finding God is like climbing a great mountain. Maybe God *is* the mountain. But suppose for a moment that God is at the top of the mountain. The enormity of the mountain is beyond all imagination. I happen to be traveling a Christian path on this great mountain of God. Why am I on this particular path? Partly because I was born along the path. Partly because the path makes sense with my experience in life. Partly because I have been nurtured on this path by the community of the church. But like many of you, I am walking and walking and walking upon this great mountain of God, this mountain of my faith journey. When you're down on the ground, the part of the mountain you are walking on seems like the whole mountain. But it's not the whole mountain at all. There is a north side and south side and east side of the mountain.

And if you were to climb into a helicopter, soar high into the sky while the whirling blades kick up little cyclones of dust, and let's say the air was not too thin to hold up the blades of the helicopter as you climbed higher and higher, and say you could have a complete aerial view of this great mountain, what you would see is that there are many Christian people following the Christian path. You also notice there are little trails leading off from the Christian path. Some are the Episcopal trail, the Presbyterian trail, the Methodist trail. There is the Baptist trail. (They actually have many trails going off from the trail going off from the Christian path.) And there are some who think their trail is the right trail, the only trail leading to the summit of God's presence.

But as you continue to gaze at the mountain, chopper blades whirling and whirling and whirling, you see there are other paths. You notice some of the mountain travelers are following a Buddhist path. You drop altitude just a little to get a good look at the pilgrims, and you notice they seem to be deeply devoted to the path they are walking. Just as devoted as the Christians walking their path. The path is a little different. The landmarks and signs are a little different. You've never seen prayer wheels before, but you do know something about prayer and the importance of it for the journey. You don't know much about meditation, but you do love your quiet time on Sunday mornings as you celebrate the eucharist. Even though there are differences on the path, you clearly see there is only one mountain. The longer you fly, the more paths you see. You notice an Islamic path. A Catholic path. You notice a Jewish path. Again, all the paths are distinctive, but all are held together by the mountain.

As you fly overhead you have two primary impressions. One is how utterly enormous the mountain is. Its presence is breathtaking. You feel the deepest of awe. In the words of Van Morrison, you feel the "inarticulate speech of the heart" stir within you. You feel wonder, but you also feel humbled in its presence. But the other impression you find yourself contemplating is how the different paths come closer and closer together the higher each path moves toward the summit of the mountain. The closer to the peak, the closer the paths become. At some point near the great summit of God all the individual paths vanish and become one. Breathless, eyes and heart wide open, standing on top of the summit, what you realize is that the point of the journey was not to glorify the path, only to follow it, walk it, experience it until you finally touch the summit, until you reach the place where the path doesn't matter. In other words, wouldn't it be marvelous if we all could become a little bit like Kelly Perkins, on top of the summit, deeply alive and full of gratitude? After all, the path is not the peak and the presence is not the path. Or again, in the words of the apostle Paul, "The imperfect passes away." Dante spoke of the time when we would arrive and the path would end.

"Could it be," I proposed to Brian that night at the party, and by this time several others who were now standing around and listening, "could it be that what we need to do is relate to one another in a way that anticipates the ultimate goal of life, namely, all people being loved by God, the God we know sometimes as mother, as father, as friend, as lover, as spirit, even as mountain? And could it be that all people can enjoy the blessing of being God's children, and all people can think of themselves as brothers and sisters of the mountain, and all people can eventually arrive at the place where they need no path?" To me, this is moving closer and closer to the vision of Christ. I also suggested, "This might be the reason why Jesus never preached a sermon about Jesus! Jesus knew that God was bigger than Jesus, and that God was bigger than the path, and that God was and is bigger than the mountain."

We are living more and more in a world that does not appreciate the experiences of others. We've become myopic in thinking that our path is the only path. Our viewpoint the only viewpoint. Our opinion the only opinion. He who shouts the loudest or makes the most appearances on *Oprah* wins the day. If a person is the "weakest link," too bad, off you go. This kind of exclusivity, especially when cloaked in religion, makes the world more dangerous for all people. There is a way, surely there is a way, to love and appreciate the Christian path we are on while at the same time opening our hearts toward those on other paths. The key is respect. Respecting the experiences of others. Respecting the journey of others. (None of us are where we are going to be!) And we respect the lives and faith of others, knowing that at the highest aspirations of faith, all the faiths of the world are moving toward that ineffable one we name God.

I've been intrigued by something Thomas Merton once wrote. Merton was a Trappist monk living most of his life in a monastery in Kentucky, but Merton was a pioneer—maybe I should say spiritual mountaineer?—who opened up a significant dialogue with people of the Buddhist faith. Not surprisingly, Merton also was severely criticized for this kind of openness. The fear was that Merton would somehow compromise the Catholic faith if he engaged in true dialogue with the Buddhists.

Merton, however, understood the depth of religious experience and the unifying power of it, so much so that he suggested that the more he became a Catholic, the more he became a Buddhist, and the more he became a Buddhist, the more he become a Catholic. I find that sentiment remarkable, not only because of the essential religious unity that Merton appreciated, but because his heart had become so open that in his experience he was able to hold many dimensions of faith. His comments are not unlike what I once heard Huston Smith say in a lecture. When asked how as a Christian he could have so much respect for other world religions, Smith said, "I will always be a Christian in my body because I was baptized. But my soul is bigger than my body, and thus my appreciation for other pathways."

The spiritual journey moves us inward to be sure, but it also moves us outward, stretching and expanding the heart like the great horizon of Montana, opening up until a rich diversity of spiritual experience finds a home within our personal experience. Not only do I feel a need for this burgeoning experience in my personal life, I'm aware that the world needs it. The fragmentation of the global family is becoming more and more intense and increasingly more violent. But to live with the kind of faith that fosters respect and peace among people, accenting the common humanity present in all religious expression, can become a world-transforming energy. Therefore, to nurture the faith of an open heart means that I have both the chance and the challenge to nurture the larger picture of humanity, infusing into humanity a spirit of tolerance, compassion, and ultimately companionship with my fellow travelers. As a Christian, I ground such openness in the story of Jesus, the man who lived radically for others, which means that if spirituality is to resonate inside my story, I too must live for others.

Now a great mountain theology, a true ecu-faith, raises all kinds of questions. What does it mean to love our neighbor? What does it mean to open our hearts to both friends and strangers, neighbors in our own churches and neighbors of different faiths on the other side of the world? And should the church be proactive in sharing the Christian story with others?

These are the faith questions that move us to consider how we think about people, treat people, talk to and about people. These are the questions that are part and parcel of what it means to believe in God. One thing that rings true again and again in the life of Jesus is that his faith in God never diminished the life of another person. For him, faith in God and faith in humanity became one. To enhance the life of another human being was to enhance the life of God, and to love God was to open the heart toward fellow human beings. Ecu-faith is opening the heart, it is recognizing that the household of humanity lives in God and God lives in the household of humanity.

I think Christians can and should tell the story of their faith, but do it in a way that is invitational. When you think about it, that is really the only way the Christian story should ever be told, given the fact that the whole life of Christ was one of inviting people to reunite with God. Furthermore, there are more and more people in our culture who are completely unconnected with *any* religious faith and, in turn, disconnected from some of their most important spiritual dimensions. Shouldn't these people be our concern and passion, not to "make" them Christians nor to "make" them like us, but inviting them to find for themselves this awesome embrace of love we have found through the story of Jesus? The word *evangelism* simply means the sharing of the good news, and in the tradition of the angels, we become angel-like by sharing the heart of God.

There's an often-told Jewish tale about a rabbi asking his students how they could tell a new day had dawned. One student replied, "Well, you can tell it is a new day when there is enough light to see the difference between an apple tree and a pear tree." It was a good answer, but not the right answer. Another student suggested, "Rabbi, you can tell it's a new day when you can look down the road and tell whether or not the animal up ahead is a fox or a dog." Again, a good answer, but not the one the rabbi was looking for. The rabbi paused for a few moments and then said to his eager students, "It's a new day when there is enough light helping you see the face of another human being, and looking upon their face you see your brother or your sister. Until that happens, it is still night."

We are all walking the great mountain of God together. Increasingly, the mountain is getting smaller and smaller because we are one click of a button away from India or China or Afghanistan. The smaller the mountain becomes, the greater the danger, but also, the greater the opportunity becomes for human community. Even as I write this paragraph, there are men and women circling the globe in an international space station. If they can achieve spatial perspective that will forever change how they imagine planet Earth, there should be a way we can gain some spiritual perspective that will enhance the human experience. I am a Christian walking the Christian path, as I assume most of you who are reading this book are too. In spite of all its shortcomings, I'm grateful for the church and the path that it continues to carve out upon the mountain. But isn't there a way to love the path we are on while appreciating and learning from those who are walking different paths? Isn't the mountain big enough for all of us? Isn't God big enough for us all too?

Sometimes I think people of religious faith, regardless of their particular path, fail to appreciate how desperately they are in need of God's healing love. We are walking the mountain path of the spirit, not because we are in some abstract sense supposed to be walking it, but because we ourselves are in need of healing. It is our own brokenness that drives us to our knees again and again. It is our own wounds, our longings and hopes, our darkness and mystery that causes us to take step after step on the spiritual journey. The mountain of God, therefore, is not merely a destination we are trying to achieve, but it is the very source of healing we need for our lives. Which means we need one another. Which means our fundamental human needs link us together. Which means that if we can share some of the healing we have found on the path, then that will only enhance the experiences of others; moreover, it will enhance our experiences too. My deepest awareness after our national tragedy on September 11, 2001, was how intensely we needed one another. You could feel it in the air. It was palpable and beautiful. But more than a response to tragedy, isn't this what God created us to be: fellow pilgrims, walking the many paths of the mountain, but knowing all along that the mountain itself is our source of life?

CHAPTER ELEVEN

The Imagination of Compassion

*One of the paradoxes of the mystical life is this: that a man
cannot enter into the deepest center of himself and pass
through that center into God, unless he is able to pass
entirely out of himself and empty himself and give himself to
other people in the purity of a selfless love.*

THOMAS MERTON[1]

Before his death a few years ago, Joseph Cardinal Bernardin
was the archbishop of Chicago. In his moving little book *The
Gift of Peace* he described one of the most painful incidents of
his life. Rumors had begun to circulate. There was a young
man, Steven Cook, and he was claiming that years ago the
archbishop, then living in Cincinnati, had sexually abused him.
Father Bernardin was stunned. He called a press conference
and categorically denied such a charge. He couldn't even
remember a Steven Cook. The questions and publicity he had
to endure during this ordeal were horrendous.

For the next one hundred days, surely the longest one
hundred days of his life, there was an investigation, and not a

little public speculation in the news media. Finally, the lawsuit was dropped, and it became clear that one of Cardinal Bernardin's harshest critics had convinced this very unhappy, very depressed young man to trump up false allegations against the archbishop. I know that clergy are not beyond making mistakes, even serious mistakes, but in this case no mistake had been made; this was nothing but a scandalous and false allegation.

What was most remarkable, however, was Cardinal Bernardin's attitude after the lawsuit had been dropped. He found himself thinking about this young man and the pain he must have felt just to initiate such a spurious proceeding. That's compassion, imagining the pain someone else is in, even when you have to transcend your own pain. Most of all, he found himself wondering about what the young man was really like as a human being. He decided to do something both bold and beautiful; he initiated a meeting with his accuser. In his own words Cardinal Bernardin describes that dramatic meeting:

> I sat with Steven on the couch…I explained to him that the only reason for requesting the meeting was to bring closure to the traumatic events of last winter by personally letting him know that I harbored no ill feelings toward him. I told him I wanted to pray for his physical and spiritual well-being. Steven replied that he had decided to meet with me so he could apologize for the embarrassment and hurt he had caused…I looked directly at Steven, seated a few inches away from me. "You know," I said, "that I never abused you."
>
> "I know," he answered softly. "Can you tell me again?"
>
> I looked directly into his eyes. "I have never abused you. You know that, don't you?"
>
> Steven nodded. "Yes," he replied, "I know that, and I want to apologize for saying that you did."
>
> Steven's apology was simple, direct, deeply moving. I accepted his apology. I told him that I had prayed for him every day.[2]

Cardinal Bernardin then gave Steven two gifts. He wasn't at all sure how they would be received, but first he gave Steven a Bible. In the front of the Bible the archbishop had inscribed a personal note. Steven took the Bible in his quivering hands and clutched it to his chest. The cardinal then gave Steven a chalice, the powerful symbol of shared life and community, symbolic of the spiritual search itself, and asked him to celebrate mass with him. And they did. Walking over to a little chapel on the campus where they were meeting, these two men shared the miracle of acceptance and holy communion. What a remarkable moment of letting go, transforming an awful experience into an experience of health and healing. To be hurt in life is part of life. To be wounded, betrayed, angry, that too is part of life. But real spiritual awakening happens when the alchemy of the imagination is brought into our life experiences. Lead becomes gold. Difficult experiences are kissed with grace. Hope and love triumph.

What's especially striking about Cardinal Bernardin's encounter is the way he assumed personal responsibility for transforming the situation. Obviously, he could have responded differently. Anger. Bitterness. Indifference. Even personal victimization. Yet what he understood and courageously put to the test was the power of God to transform even the most painful of human experiences. This is not unlike Jesus who, while being crucified on a Roman cross, cried out to God, to the universe itself, and said, "Father, forgive them for they know not what they do." This capacity to forgive, to imagine a new way of reclaiming life is part of opening the heart to God.

This kind of inspiration, the inbreathing of spirit into a situation, is desperately needed by all of us. Think of the number of times you have felt betrayed or hurt or antagonized by another person. Think of the number of times your family has disintegrated into a painful misunderstanding or an extended time of hurt feelings. Or think of the number of conflicts that occur in the workplace day after day. The human experience is peppered with all kinds of disruption, and it takes its toll on our health, our happiness, our ability to lead productive lives. Nevertheless, this downward spiral of pain does not have to be the conclusive world in which we live. The world is radically open as long as divine spirit is flowing, renewing and reclaiming our real life situations. Forgiving another person is truly a gift, not only to that person, but also to ourselves. But before we can offer such compassion, we have to imagine it.

We all have situations that demand the imagination of compassion. Some personal. Some social. But what is needed is the open heart that feels and the engaged heart that acts. Both are essential. It takes a tremendous amount of imagination to apply compassion to the world. But if we can imagine a different world, ultimately there can be a different world. Imagination is the key. The open heart moves us beyond rhetoric to a posture of respect. And then from respect, we move toward compassion. The open heart aches and acts for the common good of all people.

Compassion is more than feeling sorry for someone, and certainly more than doing an act of charity for someone in need. To feel compassion means we try to see the world, feel the world, hear the world through the experience of another. Part of the spiritual journey is coming home to ourselves and feeling the joy of life within our own skin. Another part of the spiritual journey is learning to imagine what it might be like to live inside the skin of another. Compassion creates a wonderful mingling of human experience and divine expression; for this reason, it is one of the hallmark characteristics of the Christian faith.

Jesus was forever acting with compassion. Not merely a do-gooder, Jesus allowed himself to feel the pain of a leper, or the isolation of a marginalized woman in that ancient world, or the sad loneliness of a child that transcends time and culture. Again and again he opened his heart with compassion toward others. Furthermore, he exercised compassion with a high degree of imagination. Not only could he have compassion for a tax collector, Jesus could imagine having dinner with him. Not only could he have compassion for a child, he could imagine stopping and holding a child. Not only could he have compassion and heal a leper, he could imagine the importance of touching the skin of a leper. What happened in the unfolding of his life is that, not only were others transformed by his compassion, but he himself remained forever changed by his encounters with people. We don't often think of Jesus being changed, but in fact that is part of the compelling nature of his presence. Jesus didn't just deliver messages from God; he opened himself up to other human beings—both giving and receiving—and consequently both he and the world were changed. This is the power of compassion. To open our hearts toward others always changes the world; it always changes us.

Compassion moves us in so many different directions. Sometimes it is deeply personal, supplying long-awaited healing for a family member or an important relationship. At other times, compassion heals the past by forgiving the past. Forgiveness is not easy, but without it we will reach impasse after impasse with others, even with ourselves, and such impasses will leave us stranded upon the mountain of God. At still other times, compassion is applied to larger situations, to the larger life of community, often translating into courageous acts of the spirit or small gestures of service. But before compassion can have its day in the sun, it must be invited into the realm of the heart, and more specifically, compassion must be joined with the gift of imagining a different kind of world. Imagination shouldn't be confused with make-believe. To imagine is to see new insight, to feel the experience of another, to allow something other than our personal feelings to define reality. The imagination of the heart begins to ask, "What if...What if...What if..." There is a world of difference between saying, "What if..." as opposed to saying, "Whatever..."

Compassion is the open heart taking unto itself the experiences of others, the willingness to imagine life from the inside out. Compassion is feeling, but it's more than that, it's the application of love that extends to that which we cannot understand. To only love what we understand is to love very little in life. But to love what we don't understand, that is the gift and challenge of compassion. More than what we see, more than what we experience, more than what we believe, compassion comes from the heart's acknowledging the depth of complexity in another person or situation. We sometimes say, "It's more than I can imagine!" Yet we must imagine. For to imagine the feelings and experiences of others is to open our hearts to the most sacred experience of all, namely, the experience of loving another human being.

Sometimes our moments of compassion will be fleeting. Something as simple as asking a child her name or being kind to the waitress in the restaurant or noticing the hard work of an employee. Extending compassion to the world on a daily basis is a life calling; it is spirituality in practice. Compassion can be expressed through a lifetime of "random acts of kindness." Showing respect to others is an act of compassion. Acknowledging, as I suggested earlier, that there are legitimate, authentic, albeit different spiritual paths others can follow is, in and of itself, an act of compassion. Appreciating different spiritual maps people have followed can be an act of compassion. Compassion extends itself like that great arch towering above the city of St. Louis, stretching across childhood, adolescence, adulthood, old age. Most of us are in constant need of imagining how to apply compassion to a member of our family, past or present, or to a friend or a colleague, or even to the person who cuts us off in rush hour traffic. (That's a tough one!) Compassion is positive, creative, imaginative thinking on behalf of others.

On June 10, 1996, a bullet was fired at the corner of Clark and Howard streets in the city of Chicago. It ripped through the body of a handsome man by the name of Andrew Young. He died on the street. He was nineteen years old. The killer, Mario Ramos, thought Andrew was a member of a rival gang and pulled the trigger of a semiautomatic handgun. After the killing, the story starting taking predictable turns. Andrew was not a member of any gang. He was simply a young man in the wrong place at the wrong time. He came from a remarkably close family. He was the son of Maurine Young, a woman of extraordinary strength and courage. The young man who fired the gun, Mario Ramos, a tragic figure in his own right, is now serving a life sentence in an Illinois state prison.

However, after the funeral and intense grieving, after the trial and the sentencing, Maurine Young continued to feel mysteriously incomplete. To be sure, nothing would replace her son. To be sure, she would never be the same again. Yet there was something strangely missing, and what was missing was forgiveness. She started to imagine the broken world of Mario Ramos. She started to imagine what she might say to him, what she could say to him, if she were to contact him. And then one day she wrote a letter:

> Dear Mario:
>   You don't know me, though I suspect you've heard of me. I am Andrew's mom. I've thought of you and prayed for you many times since the day you shot and killed my son...I don't know whether you feel up to asking my forgiveness, so I'll go first. I forgive you.

Candidly, my first reaction as I read this story from the *Chicago Tribune* was "I can't imagine; I can't imagine her grief, I can't imagine losing a child, I can't imagine her contacting her son's killer." Imagine is exactly what Maurine Young did. Compassion is always rooted in imagination. But more than a written letter, a few years later, after many letters had been exchanged between Maurine and Mario, she went to the prison in order to meet him face-to-face. She recalls the first time she sat down across from Mario and took his trembling hands in her own, and said to him, "Mario, you came into my life through a violent action, but now I embrace you as my son. You are now part of this family, and you have the responsibility to hold our family in prayer."

Sometimes compassion is reaching new vistas of understanding, but at times something more than understanding is called for; sometimes the only way to reclaim experience is through the gift of forgiveness. Don't let that word *gift* fool you. Forgiveness is hard work. Rarely is it easy. Notwithstanding, when it happens, when it touches real human experience, it is something of a miracle, but it never happens without the imagination of compassion. If spirituality is the journey of opening up our spirit to the spirit of God, then there can be no better pathway to walk than the pathway of imagining compassion. It is the essence of God and, therefore, the essence of life. Cardinal Bernardin. Maurine Young. These are simple ordinary/extraordinary people who allowed something big and deep and mysterious to flow through their lives like a great river, like a great Mississippi River of divine influence. How lovely, how needed, how essential is that river named compassion.

One perspective that seems to be growing with clarity these days regarding the life of Jesus is that he arrived, not to tear down Judaism per se, but to challenge a particular kind of community politic, a politic characterized by adherence to religious purity laws. I will say more about this shortly, but let it suffice for now to point out that at the heart of Jesus' life was the release of divine compassion for the world, including but not limited to the gift of forgiveness. We never become more Christlike than when we share the gift of forgiveness with others. It's troubling to me when some people try to take a Christianity of grace and compassion and turn it into a system of obedience and oppression, turning it into the very system of religion that Jesus was trying to overturn in the first place. At the heart of Judaism is God's steadfast love, and at the heart of Christianity is God's grace. If these great faiths respectively started with the release of God's compassion and love, then it only makes sense that they should continue to exist for the very same purposes. I can only speak for the church, mind you, but I'm confident in saying that often the church has needed to be less like the church and more like the Christ who inspired the church. Nowhere is this more true than in our calling to share the gift of compassion with others.

The compassionate imagination is important not only because it represents the quintessential center of the Christian faith but also because of what it means for the well-being of the human family. No one has been a more articulate spokesman in recent years on the topic of compassion than the Dalai Lama. In a recent essay he piles image upon image as he tries to capture the significance of compassion. "A mind committed to compassion is like an overflowing reservoir—a constant source of energy, determination, and kindness. Or this mind can be likened to a seed; when cultivated, it gives rise to many other qualities, such as tolerance, inner strength, and the confidence to overcome fear and insecurity. The compassionate mind is also like an elixir: it is capable of transforming bad situations into beneficial ones. Therefore, we should not limit our expressions of love and compassion to our family and friends.

Nor is compassion only the responsibility of clergy or health-care or social workers. It is the necessary business of every part of the human community."[3]

The imagination of compassion is essential for our lives and world. The magnification of compassion rings true with Jesus' vision of life. And in the deepest place of the soul, when expressed and shared, it affirms again why we are human beings, connected to one another and created in the image of God.

CHAPTER TWELVE

The Wondrous Christ-Burst!

As a magnifying glass concentrates the rays of the sun into a little burning knot of heat that can set fire to a dry leaf or a piece of paper, so the mystery of Christ in the Gospel concentrates the rays of God's light and fire to the point that sets fire to the spirit of people.

THOMAS MERTON[1]

Bang! That's how it all started. One great, wild, creative, erotic cosmic explosion. The combustion of matter and energy projecting particles of dust into the atmosphere, flying at unprecedented speed, the stuff of life coming together in patterned beauty and elegance into one cataclysmic biological moment. Called the Big Bang theory, it is virtually now accepted, not as a theory but as a fact, when it comes to explaining the origins of the universe.

Scientists are now able to start with what is, the present reality of earthly existence, and work backwards; in essence, they are mapping the universe. What it also means is that everything we see, touch, hear, and smell, everything from the great mountains of the Colorado Rockies to the minuscule molecules that constitute our wondrous bodies, all of it possesses the original explosive matter of the universe. The creative origins of the universe are inside all things, and all things are related to that one origin. If the universe started with that one great starburst, then it is also true that the stardust is inside all things. Everything is linked in the great web of life. This is true of human species as well as all things physical in the world: plants, animals, mountains, oceans, deserts.

On one side of faith's fault line are those who claim the world started exactly as it is portrayed in the book of Genesis. That, of course, comes from a literal approach to the Bible, believing the Bible to be a newspaper account of what really happened in the beginning. On the other side of the fault line are those who claim that Genesis is true, not just literally true, it is poetically true, mythically true, it is deeply and profoundly true as a theological statement, but it's just not scientifically true. I don't want to argue the point, though it's worthy of exploration in that it reveals this theological fault line I've mentioned throughout the book. Instead, I want to suggest that this original starburst might be an appropriate *metaphor* for understanding the life and significance of Jesus.

Who was Jesus? What was he about? What did he say and do and believe? Like the Genesis creation stories, there are certain "accounts" of the life of Jesus found in the books of Matthew, Mark, Luke, and John. But again, even a cursory look at these four gospels suggests it would be a mistake to read them literally, trying to piece together the true historical Jesus like an airtight investigative FBI file. It's fair to make certain claims about Jesus. Who he was and what he taught, moreover, locating the force of his life and the significance of it today, is an enterprise worth engaging. But rather than starting with this historical exploration, I want to suggest that we can build the map of his life backward, that is, we can start with the Christ and the experience of Christ energy, and then move backward to the man Jesus.

Christ was not Jesus' last name. Nor was it merely a title he wore. Doctor. Reverend. Cardinal. Christ is in fact much bigger, much more expansive and explosive than any individual person. Christ is that great cosmic energy of God. Christ is divine energy, creative energy, the transforming energy of divine love. It's not that Jesus *was* the Christ, though I understand what people mean when they say he was the Christ, it's more like Christ energy had come to live and dwell and sizzle inside the historical life of Jesus. Christ is bigger than Jesus. Just as the Word is bigger than Jesus. Christ is more expansive than Jesus, than the church, than the Bible, than even our concepts of Christ. What a mistake it would be to assume that any theory about Christ is the same as Christ.

Through Jesus, Christ energy was released into the world, and that can be seen again and again in the gospels, not to mention what has been experienced personally by Christians in the life of faith. Or to follow the metaphor of the Big Bang, what happened in the life of Jesus is that there was a God-burst, a Christ-burst if you will, and the very Christ energy that had come to live inside his remarkable life exploded into the world through his living and dying and rising, and there is still pulsating through the world this energy of Christ, an energy that emanates from this original God blast.

Just as the original stardust of the universe can be said to be present in all things, so also Christ-dust. Christ energy is present in all things, creative, transforming love is present in all things, and in fact, all things are holy because Christ energy is present. To understand this Christ-burst is to open up to a new reverence for life, for ourselves, our neighbors in the world, for the world itself. This means that Jesus is not merely a figure of the past, though understanding some of his past is essential and not a little bit fascinating. The Jesus of the past continues in the world because of the presence of the indwelling energy of Christ. The spiritual journey for Christians, therefore, becomes twofold. We certainly admire Jesus because of his openness to and his imparting of Christ to the world, so at the same time, our spiritual opportunity is to welcome this Christ into our historical lives. That's what we need to do. That is what God wants us to do. The word often used to describe this process is *incarnation*. Incarnation is the process of God's essence, God's energy becoming part of our human experience.

One of the stories in the gospels that illustrates this cosmic, transforming quality of Christ energy is about Jesus going up to the mountaintop, and there with his inner circle of disciples, Peter, James, and John, he is transfigured. I imagine the day was going along like most days. That's when epiphanies happen, those moments in which we really sense the presence of God and the welcome of Christ energy into our lives. Epiphanies tend to happen when we least expect them. They come as surprise and wonder, like little electrical impulses of inspiration. Therefore, on this day in the life of Jesus, he suggests to Peter, James, and John that they go for a hike up the mountain, up the rocky, dusty mountain, through the olive groves, past all the prattle of daily activity, and there on top of the mountain they would open their hearts and minds and souls to the presence of God in prayer. This was SOP for Jesus. Standard Operating Procedure. Or maybe I should say it looked like it was SOP. It looked like yesterday and today and tomorrow.

Yet if faith teaches us anything at all, it is that the ordinary can quickly become the extraordinary, that the mundane can become sacred with the mere blink of an eye, and that the profane can become holy with only the slightest of shift in perspective. Life is not always what it appears to be, which of course is very good news for most of us. After all, we all have circumstances in life that are difficult and painful, or we face futures that seem bleak and hopeless, like driving down a dead-end street. Yet part of the energy of Christ is that there is more to the world, and therefore more to our lives, than meets the eye.

I love it that Jesus goes to the mountaintop, for there he would risk the experience of faith himself. (Maybe he knew the mountain was the source for his healing, too.) He would open himself to God, he would pray and reflect and quiet his soul, and there he would open up his heart so wide that the presence of God would flow within him. True faith is always an existential decision. Always. It was for Jesus, for as he climbed that mountain with his disciples, he was exhibiting spiritual daring and courage. As I have suggested throughout this book, the true nature of faith is to be on a journey. Jesus did not arrive merely to explain the journey or to deliver a rule book about how to find God. He led people to God by trying to find God himself.

As the story is told, Jesus was transfigured by the presence of God. He became dazzling with light. So transparent was he that something of the presence of God started to glow within him. And if all that wasn't enough, it looked as if, hard to tell, but it looked as if two of the great figures of Jewish history also appeared at his side, Moses and Elijah, as if to suggest that just as God had worked through these great religious leaders in the past, now God is working through the life of Jesus in the present. This is in no way a repudiation of these powerful Jewish leaders. Actually, it's more of a continuation of the work of God in the world. Christ energy has always been and is always being incarnated into the world. This mountaintop moment was a transfiguration.

I like the dramatic details of the story, but the details aren't given so much to tell exactly what happened on top of that mountain as they are designed to suggest what is possible for spiritual life today. Another word for transfiguration is transformation. That's what God is about. God is about creative transformation. God is about loving transformation. And transformation is the essence of Christ. Jesus was transfigured, transfigured in the sense of being transformed by something that transcended his day-to-day living, transfigured in the sense that on top of that mountain, in that particular moment, in that sacred place and time he was transformed by Christ energy that assured him he was loved and accepted by God.

And here's the point of the biblical story. Just as there was a dramatic confluence of Christ energy within Jesus, could it be that divine love, could divine creativity and divine acceptance come so close to your life and my life, so near to the old bones of our lives, could divine reality that we understand as infinite grace and inexhaustible wonder, could that peace that passes all understanding drift down toward our lives the way clouds settle on mountain peaks? Could that one who is above all and in all and through all, could that kind of spiritual immediacy come so close that it might transfigure/transform human life today? Jesus had his epiphanies, moments of remarkable clarity into Christ energy, as at his baptism, as on this mountaintop; Jesus had his epiphanies, not so we would frame him with our admiration, but so we could see that such moments are possible for us. If we really admire Jesus, if we really want to honor him with our lives, we will risk the same journey he risked, opening ourselves to the incarnation of divine energy within our experience. In the end, if incarnation only belongs to Jesus, then our own humanity is as hollow as Mammoth Cave.

There's an interesting fresco in a Roman catacomb that pictures Christ as universal, cosmic energy. It dates to approximately 350 C.E. In this remarkable painting the figure of Jesus is presented front and center surrounded by the disciples. A typical scene. His right hand is raised, extended as a gesture of communication. He wears a white garment. The disciples look very young in comparison with the Christ figure. Jesus is no longer the shepherd in this artistic rendition, but is painted as a teacher, instructor, even ruler. But immediately behind him are two figures, angelic in appearance, and they are holding up a dark blue, almost indigo colored cape. Scattered upon the blue field of the cape are shining stars. Fascinating. The cosmos is now a beautiful cape, and the angelic figures are about to place the cape upon Jesus, the cape of the universe, suggesting that Jesus is much more than Jesus, he is the cosmic Christ that has touched the entire web of life. The world came into being through a starburst! And in Jesus what has taken place is nothing less than a Christ-burst.

Men and women today are able to experience the cosmic quality of Christ by appreciating the great mystery of life. Original goodness is in all things. This is a far different starting point than some presentations of the Christian faith where the emphasis is on the depravity of the world and is therefore suspicious of all things, especially things that bring pleasure to the body! If Christ energy is in the world, then that means there is a certain artistry to life, a poetry to life and, in turn, that means wonder and awe and reverence are essential characteristics of the spiritual journey. Playfulness is important. Eroticism is important, not just sexuality, but seeing that there is an erotic energy that fills the universe. It also means that every Christian should cultivate his or her inner mystic. Mysticism is simply living life with the conviction that the physical world is possessed by inner meaning. The Jesus who wears the cape of sky and stars and planets is not the same one who walked the dusty roads of Israel. Instead, something much more expansive has exploded through his life, a Christ explosion of love and life and creativity. The apostle Paul wrote to a congregation of Christians, actually prayed for them that "Christ might be formed" in them. What could such a notion of Christ being formed in us mean? I think Paul was touching upon this marvelous experience of allowing the energies of Christ to become incarnated within our lives and allowing our lives to become carriers of Christ.

It is precisely this reality of transformation I felt when I recently read about a woman who was very ill, in the last stages of dying with AIDS. She was at home. Very depressed. Very discouraged. A friend reached out to her and called her priest to come by and see her. The woman candidly confessed to the priest, "I've made a mess of my life. I've made so many mistakes. How could God forgive me?"

The priest said, "God can forgive anyone. Anytime. We just have to trust it. Receive it. Let it come close."

The woman said, "I think I'm beyond believing it."

At that very moment the priest happened to notice that on the woman's dresser in her bedroom was picture of a beautiful young girl. Maybe she was twelve years old. He asked her, "Who is that girl in the picture?"

For the first time in the conversation the woman flashed a smile and said, "Oh, that's my daughter. She is the only beautiful thing in my life."

The priest said, "And if your daughter made some mistakes and did some things that were wrong and was hurting and broken, wouldn't you forgive her, wouldn't you come close to her and still love her?"

The woman, whispering now, said, "Yes. Yes. Yes, of course."

And then that priest made a wonderful, theologically astute connection. He said, "I want you to know that God has a picture of *you* on God's dresser. And God loves you."

Such love, such compassion, such presence coming near to our lives, even as it came near to Jesus on top of that mountain, is nothing less than the essence of Christ drawing near to us. It is an epiphany when we can finally believe that there is a picture of me and a picture of you on God's dresser, that we are children of God. That God wants to come as close to our lives as God came to the life of Jesus. We may not be transfigured, but we will be transformed. That's what love does. That's what Christ does. It always changes us. None of us will ever become *the* Christ. Such designation is for Jesus and Jesus only. But we can participate in the very energies of Christ, the particles of the original Christ-burst still glowing in our lives through faith.

One concluding detail from this transfiguration story of Jesus. It's interesting to me that the disciples, Peter, James, and John, when in the presence of the transforming power of God wanted somehow to contain it, enclose it, make it tied to one place and time. Elijah appears. Moses appears. Jesus appears. But the disciples, in awe to be sure, wanted to hold it all by building little booths for worship. On the one hand, their attitude is admirable. When in awe, worship! On the other hand, Christ energy cannot be tied down. It is too wild and numinous. It is too strong and active. Christ energy cannot be tied to a mountain, nor can it even be tied to the historical figure of Jesus. In Jesus, the Christ-burst happened, but in people who continue to follow Jesus, the Christ-burst continues to erupt and explode. It's the nature of God. Therefore, the church is called, not to hold this energy, but to release it, share it, spread it around and give it to others through authentic religious words and actions, through hope shared and compassion implemented, through a community of people called the body of Christ.

CHAPTER THIRTEEN

The Many Faces of Jesus

Regardless of what anyone may personally think or believe about him, Jesus of Nazareth has been the dominant figure in the history of Western culture for almost twenty centuries. If it were possible, with some sort of super-magnet, to pull up out of that history every scrap of metal bearing at least a trace of his name, how much would be left? It is from his birth that most of the human race dates its calendars, it is by his name that millions curse and in his name that millions pray.

JAROSLAV PELIKAN[1]

My grandfather Gayle was the kind of man who had a passion for life. He was the life of the party, loved practical jokes, and delighted in relentlessly teasing people. But he also loved gadgets. One of my most vivid memories is that my grandfather had the very first Polaroid camera I had ever seen. Of course I had seen regular, ordinary cameras, the kind of cameras that required you to take the film down to the drugstore and wait for a week or more to get the pictures developed, but the Polaroid camera, now that was a completely different story.

Compared to the camcorders and digital cameras of today, I'm sure it was a clumsy kind of contraption, but at that time, the Polaroid camera represented cutting-edge technology. You would load the film, pull the lens apparatus out on an accordion-like extender, and then you would snap the picture. The fascinating part was that you would then pull out one frame of the film from the back of the camera. And then you would watch the film develop. I remember the burning curiosity of watching and waiting for the film to develop, watching it before my very eyes, watching it as if it were magic. Sometimes we would wave the picture in the air, holding it between the thumb and index finger, thinking that it would help make it develop faster. Did it help? I don't think it had anything to do with making it work faster or better, but we still waved the film and moved it through the air. But after a period of time, I don't remember exactly how long, the picture would appear.

At first you could just see some ghostlike figure of white light. And then the person came more and more into focus. Soon you could see the face, the body, the arms, the legs, and if you waited long enough, you could see the eyes, the ears, and then the most important part of the picture, you could see the smile. But before the picture could be enjoyed, there was that significant Polaroid experience of waiting, the time in-between taking the picture and getting to see the picture, that time of developing, that time of coming into focus, that time when you are seeing but you're not quite sure what you're going to see. Or maybe you can think about it like this: There is a time when someone may be sending you an e-mail, maybe with an elaborate document or even photographs or sound, but before you get to the point of clarity, you have to wait for the downloading. Different speed, perhaps, than an old Polaroid camera, but it still requires watching and waiting.

In many ways, all we have today of Jesus are Polaroid snapshots. Some are a little clearer than others. Some are a little blurry. A few have surprising clarity. Still others continue to develop even though the actual photograph was taken over 2,000 years ago. To make it even more challenging, sometimes when we read one of the four gospels what we're seeing is not merely a photograph of Jesus but a photographic overlay that has been placed upon the picture of Jesus, an overlay that reflects more of what was going on at the end of the first century with the church and the writer of the gospel than what was going on with Jesus himself. That is to say, there is layer upon layer upon layer over any picture of Jesus. Even the inside of our own experience, called perspective, that we use as we look at the pictures becomes a layer of our understanding of Jesus.

I want to suggest that there are coherent snapshots that begin to emerge about Jesus presenting not just one, but many faces of Jesus. There was a complexity to his life, but that complexity is positive and rich, for it gives us not a flat, one-dimensional Jesus, but a Jesus that is rich and full, a Jesus that can speak to the world and our lives in a variety of ways.

My concern as I look on both sides of the fault line running through Protestantism today is that some want a flat Jesus, a one-dimensional Jesus. Moreover, it is a Jesus that seems to have utter clarity and focus. No mystery. No ambiguity. No complexity. This isn't merely a simple Jesus, for indeed he seemed to be possessed with a simplicity that was in and of itself compelling, but there is a huge difference between a simple Jesus and a simplistic Jesus. A simple Jesus? Yes. But a simplistic Jesus? No. I suppose there are many reasons why Jesus still matters after 2,000 years of history have passed under the bridge of human experience, but surely one reason is because there is a depth to Jesus that is never exhausted. Like a great work of art, every time you look at Jesus you can see something new, experience some new insight. He is like a great piece of music: every time you listen to his life you can discover some new layer of meaning. Therefore, my hope is that people can move closer and closer to embracing and being embraced by a more complex Jesus. A Jesus with many faces.

What might this Polaroid montage look like?

One photograph, and yes, the very first photograph I would include in this montage is that of the Jewish face of Jesus. Woodenly put, Jesus was not a Christian. He didn't come to start a new Christian religion. He didn't come to abolish Judaism. He didn't come to bring a superior way to God. He didn't come to reject Jewish people, nor is it accurate to say that he was rejected by the Jewish people, even though this is often proposed as a line of reasoning by some Christians. Furthermore, he didn't come to get rid of Jewish customs and practices. The conflicted ways in which Jesus is portrayed in the gospels vis-à-vis the Jews reflects more the conflict of the synagogue and the Gentile church at the end of the first century than it does with what was happening with Jesus. Jesus was first and foremost a man of the Torah and, in turn, a man of the Jewish experience. It was his custom, for example, to go to the synagogue for worship. He was nurtured by such practices. Nurtured and shaped by Jewish scriptures and stories. He observed Jewish holidays and followed Jewish teachings. Every teaching of Jesus, so far as I can tell, germinated and was rooted in some corner of the garden of Judaism.

Why is it so important to see this Jewish face of Jesus? There are probably several reasons, but one has to do with the very culture in which we live. We live in a society that desperately wants spiritual experience, but people want it without being connected to any reservoir of spiritual tradition. I hear this sentiment again and again when people say, "I'm not very religious, but I am deeply spiritual." There's a sense in which I'm sure this is true. I don't need to judge people about what they feel in their hearts. At the same time, there are great spiritual traditions and communities of faith of which Judaism and Christianity are just two, and these traditions have the power to deepen and inform the spiritual journey. Indeed, part of spirituality is being connected to something bigger than yourself; it's a spiritual feeling that is near to our bones, but it is also a feeling that is majestic and transcendent. The Jewish Jesus becomes a vivid reminder that spirituality needs grounding in some kind of larger tradition.

There's another reason, however, why this Jewish dimension of Jesus is so important to appreciate. When Jesus is cut out of his historical context the way we might clip a coupon out of a magazine, it then becomes far too easy to develop an anti-Jewish outlook on faith. Sadly, Christians have done this for centuries. Sometimes unwittingly, at other times consciously and maliciously. Part of the historical reckoning now taking place within the Christian tradition is that there has been a steady stream of anti-Jewish teaching flowing from the church;

in turn this has created a climate of anti-Judaism, in turn creating all kinds of ill treatment toward the Jews, in turn making possible the most horrible human tragedy in modern times, the Holocaust.

To see the Jewish face of Jesus is to learn to appreciate not only the beauty and complexity of Judaism but also the historical evolution of the Christian faith. In its earliest years, the Christian faith grew from Judaism, not against it but from it, and such recognition is healthy for both Christians and Jews. Furthermore, the Christian faith does not have to find its validity for existence by defining itself over against Judaism. In a much more positive way, Christians can appreciate that in the life of Jesus they have come to know God through the Christ energy released into the world, but even the concept of *Christ* is completely Jewish in origin. *Christ* simply means to pour oil on a person's head, anointing a king or Jewish ruler. To be the Christ was a metaphoric way of saying that this one, this individual, had been anointed by God. This is only another reminder of how much Jesus and the faith that developed around him was beholden to Judaism. Christians celebrate the creative, transforming love they have found through the presence of Christ, but Christ came to the world through the historical Jewish experience of Jesus.

There are other faces of Jesus, however: the face of compassion, the face of love, the face of hope. But all of these faces reflect what was no doubt one of the most compelling faces of Jesus, the face of acceptance. Jesus pushed open the boundaries of acceptance toward human beings in ways that challenged both religious and secular culture, an acceptance that is still compelling and troubling today.

One of my favorite stories of Jesus has to do with Zacchaeus, and it's a favorite partly because I think it's a fundamental human need to find the face of divine acceptance. Perhaps the best way into the story of Zacchaeus is through a poem by Mary Oliver entitled "The Swan." The swan is large. White. Graceful. I want you to go down to the shore of a lake, see the water gently lapping against the shore, smell the plants and water, notice how the light shimmers on the surface of the lake. And then see the swan out on the quiet lake moving toward

the shore, moving slowly, indolently, moving toward the shore.
You watch the swan. It's hypnotic. Mesmerizing. You can't take
your eyes off it. But as the swan comes closer, you begin to
realize that this swan is not just coming toward the shore, but
it's coming to you, as if it has some message for you, some gift
for you, and you keep watching and watching, watching the
swan draw near to you. Enjoy the poem.

Across the wide waters
    something comes
        floating–a slim
            and delicate

ship, filled
    with white flowers–
        and it moves
            on its miraculous muscles

as though time didn't exist,
    as though bringing such gifts
        to the dry shore
            was a happiness

almost beyond bearing.
    And now it turns its dark eyes,
        it rearranges
            the clouds of its wings,

it trails
    an elaborate webbed foot,
        the color of charcoal.
            Soon it will be here.

Oh, what shall I do
    when that poppy-colored beak
        rests in my hand?
            Said Mrs. Blake of the poet:

I miss my husband's company–
    he is so often
        in paradise.
            Of course! the path to heaven

doesn't lie down in flat miles.
It's in the imagination
with which you perceive
this world,

and the gestures
with which you honor it.
Oh, what will I do, what will I say, when those
white wings
touch the shore?[2]

Aren't we all looking for the swan? All of us? We are all looking for some gesture of God to swim close to us. Some divine inkling. Some Polaroid picture of God to develop. We are looking for some sign, if you will, a sign that confirms our deepest hope that we matter as human beings in this world, that says to us in one way or another, "I love you. The heart of the universe is open to you. This world is not hostile toward you. You are welcomed into the home of yourself, to the home of others; you are welcomed to the home of my presence." We want to go down to the lake and look out at the water; or we want to sit down in the quiet of the kitchen early in the morning and drink our coffee; or we want to drive to work, but instead of turning the radio on, we just want to think and think and think; or we want to come into a sanctuary on a Sunday morning, and what we want is some thought, some feeling, some message that says to us, "I am God and I accept you." When we really feel God's welcome and celebration and acceptance of our lives, it is as beautiful and mysterious and wondrous as a swan swimming toward us and touching our dry shore with its wings.

Zacchaeus, oh Zacchaeus must have had the feeling that this man walking down the streets of Jericho was, well, was swanlike. He must have felt as if something was coming close to the dry shore of his life. It was Jesus of Nazareth to be sure, but Jesus was representing something bigger than Jesus. He was wearing the face of divine acceptance. That's why he is called the Son of God. To say Jesus was the Son of God is a metaphoric way of saying that in the historical life of Jesus the presence of God was carried to the world.

The world had not been a welcoming place for Zacchaeus. He was a chief tax collector, and he was rich. Which is a way of saying that he was a Jewish man working for the Roman government, and the fact that he was rich, at least in this context, suggests that he had defrauded people in his effort to accumulate his massive wealth. He wasn't accepted by the Jewish community because he was working for Rome. He wasn't accepted by the Roman community because he was Jewish. He wasn't accepted by the poor because he levied higher and higher taxes upon them. He wasn't accepted by other tax collectors because they all knew that they were all frauds, and you can't trust a fraud.

Zacchaeus was a lonely man living in a threatening and hostile world. But he had heard something—what, I'm not exactly sure—but he had heard something about Jesus. Okay, you remember the Bible school song, "Zacchaeus was a wee little man and a wee little man was he." Let's just leave it like this to be politically correct at the beginning of the twenty-first century, "Zacchaeus was vertically challenged!" But in fact his real challenge was not the size of his body, it was the emptiness of his heart. And that's probably true for a lot of us. Something was missing. Something was askew. Yes, he had money. Yes, he was making a living. But there was still something missing. That wee little man climbed up a sycamore tree, his little squirrel legs shimmying up the trunk, his soft, childlike hands grabbing on to the branches, the bark scratching the inside of his legs, the prickly branches cutting up his ankles, his hands, sweat dripping down his round, empty, pasty little face. Ah, he climbed up that sycamore tree just to get a glimpse of a swan coming down the street. A glimpse of the face of Jesus.

Jesus had two options at this point in his encounter with Zacchaeus. One option was to preach a sermon. Granted, he would have had to look up the whole time, maybe even cupping his hands and raising his voice so that Zacchaeus could hear point one, point two, point three. He could have said something like all things find their being in God, could have said something about God being the perfect receiver of all imperfect people, could have said something like the heart is restless until it finds its home in God, he could have given a sermon. Well, to be honest, Jesus could have given a brilliant theological lecture on the divine reality that is in all and above all, complete with footnotes and appendices. He could have done that. I would have loved reading that sermon; but here's the point, Jesus did not do that. What Jesus understood was that religion is more about gesture than explanation, more about poetry than proclamation, and the best of religion is more about the faces you see than the words coming from those faces.

Instead of preaching, he opens wide his swanlike arms, cranes his neck slightly upward, and then says to this wee little man hanging from the branches like a Koala bear, "Zacchaeus, I would like to go home with you today." A gesture of acceptance—emotional, physical, psychological, spiritual—is always more powerful than a sermon about acceptance. The gift Jesus was carrying inside his body was that God loves us and receives us and accepts us as men and women. We don't have to loathe ourselves. We don't have to be defensive in a hostile world. We don't have to put others down to make ourselves look better. We don't have to exclude others in order to feel included ourselves. We don't have to be better than what we really are. We don't have to earn a spot in God's favor. We don't have to live with nagging self-doubt and self-disdain.

What Jesus did with Zacchaeus, not in a sermon, not in a lecture, but in one powerful gesture of the gospel, was to reveal that, at the heart of the universe, there is divine acceptance.

Henri Nouwen once said "Our biggest fear is that we will not be accepted."[3] I think he was right. It begins at birth when we pop out into the world, and we wonder if we will be accepted by a mother or a father, and that fear lasts until we draw our final breath upon this Earth. What Jesus was and is trying to bring to the world is a profound and mystical sense of God's radical acceptance. We already know that we make mistakes. We already know that we fall short of God. There's nothing new to that story. We know that the world can be a hostile, threatening place. Everything from the weather, to a company shutting down, to a dreaded disease communicates that message. We know how hard finding acceptance in relationships can be. But there is a face of Jesus, partly a Jewish face suggesting he was grounded in history, community, and tradition, and partly a face of acceptance, suggesting that God says yes to our lives.

I wasn't there, of course, but I have a hunch that when Zacchaeus looked down from that sycamore tree, looking at the face of Jesus, hearing those words about going to his house for dinner that night, I have a hunch that what he saw was a face as mystical and beautiful and welcoming as any he had ever seen before in his life. There were many faces that Jesus flashed toward the world. But it really comes down to this. There was something earthly and historical about his face. His face was in the moment. Which is why Christianity can never be reduced to a mere philosophy of life. There was something incarnational about the face of Jesus. But there is another dimension, namely, that the historical face of Jesus allowed the expression of the Christ-burst. That's why for many of us through the centuries, for someone wearing loneliness upon his back like Zacchaeus, to see the face of Jesus is to see love, grace, acceptance. I don't know, I wasn't there, mind you, but somehow I think the face of Jesus must have appeared to Zacchaeus as lovely, well, as lovely as a swan.

CHAPTER FOURTEEN

The Welcome Table of the Spirit

It was late and dark when I got there after a long bus ride, but there were lights on in the house. My wife and daughter were there. They had waited supper for me. There was a fire in the woodstove, and the cat was asleep on his back in front of it, one paw in the air. There are problems at home for all of us—problems as dark in their way as the dark streets of any city—but they were nowhere to be seen just then. There was nothing there just then except stillness, light, peace, and love that had brought me back again and that I found waiting for me when I got there.

FREDERICK BUECHNER[1]

I was a kid at Cub Scout camp. Well, to call it *camp* is a bit of an exaggeration. It was just a weekend camping trip about twenty-three-and-a-half miles from my house. I lived in Salem, Indiana. The camp was in Mitchell, Indiana. The camp facilities were, as they say, "charmingly rustic." The truth is, they were the pits. I remember thinking that I wanted to go to the camp, that I should want to go to the camp, that it would be fun if I would go on this Cub Scout weekend with all my other friends. On the other hand, I didn't much like being away from home. And I really wasn't that adventurous. And I was having a few deep existential doubts, at least as deep as they can be for a ten-year-old about to leave home for the weekend.

I went on the campout.

I did all right in the late afternoon. Did all right at dinner. Did all right at the campfire. But when it was time to go to bed, I started missing home. All I could think about was going home. All I could think about was my mom and dad and my own bedroom. I thought about my place. My home. My space in life. And so, I did the only thing a good Cub Scout could do. I lied. Oh, to call it a lie is too strong a word; I creatively told the truth. I told my scout leader that I was feeling sick. He said, "Well, where does it hurt?" I said, "I think it's my head and my stomach, well, I think it hurts everywhere!" He said, "Why don't you just try to go to sleep?"

At that moment I became the most disappointing Cub Scout in the history of Cub Scouts. Right there in that dingy dormitory, dark as dark can be, I started to cry in front of my Cub Scout leader. The events have blurred through the years. Somebody helped me pack. A call was made. I waited at that charmingly rustic lodge. And pretty soon I saw the headlights of a car coming down the lane, and then it stopped, and then out walked my dad. I don't think I've ever been happier than I was at that moment when I saw my dad.

This is what I remember—simple things—but this is what I remember after he arrived that night. I remember he said, "I hear you're not feeling well. Why don't you just come home with me?" He knew I was homesick. I knew I was homesick. I don't remember anything that was said on that twenty-three-and-a-half-mile trip back home, but I never felt like he was upset with me, disappointed with me, annoyed with me. He may have been, but I never felt it. And when we got home, miraculously, I made a medical comeback. I bounced back like a spiked volleyball, because the other thing I remember his saying after we were back home, back in my home, back in the place where I belonged, was, "Why don't I fix a pizza and we'll watch *The Tonight Show*?" I was never so glad in all my life to see Johnny Carson as I was that night. The pizza tasted so good. I was home. The pizza was my little communion, and I was home.

There is hardly a more sacred moment than when we feel ourselves at home, which is why for Christians one of the most sacred moments in the faith experience is when the eucharist is shared in the midst of the church. There are so many different ways of thinking about communion, and it's not that any one of them is necessarily wrong, it's just that there is no one image that can exhaust this powerful ritual.

Two words, however, capture the essence of this welcome table of the Spirit. One of course is *communion*. Communion is a time of entering into a mystical union with the presence of Christ, the living presence of Christ that still pulsates from the Christ-burst that took place in the historical experience of Jesus centuries ago. When I think of communion, I think of that experience of being at one with something, allowing it to get inside your bones, under your skin, feeling wonderfully connected to it. Communion is a feeling mode about a place or a person or even an idea. It implies a certain degree of intimacy. Even sexual intimacy can be a certain kind of communion, feeling at one with another person. Sometimes communion is physical. Sometimes it's spiritual. Sometimes it's both. In the act of sharing bread and wine at the table of God, there is a communion that is felt toward God, but it also moves out horizontally toward a communion with others. It becomes a very simple ritual of remembering that just as Christ-love is within me, it is also within others, and therefore the whole experience of communion with Christ becomes an experience of communion with other human beings.

But communion is also *eucharist,* a time of giving thanks for the greatest gift any of us will ever know, the gift of love. Being in the presence of a love that was embodied in the life of Jesus creates an omnivorous sense of gratitude. It really can't be overstated how essential gratitude is for the well-being of our lives. When we are grateful, simply put, we are alive. When we are not grateful, we are dead. Again, like the feelings of communion, feelings and thoughts of thanksgiving move vertically as well as horizontally. In a vertical direction (knowing there is really no spatial direction for God; God is always true center) we are grateful for the gift of God's love that was embodied in the life of Jesus, a love that became bigger than Jesus, a creative, transforming love that is sometimes called the Christ. In a horizontal direction, love connects us to one another, causing us to be thankful for one another. Or as one of the great hymns of the church reminds us, "All who live in love are thine."

One way to appreciate the significance of this welcome table of communion is to see that it symbolizes so much more than what it appears. It is true that communion is a sacrament of the church. But viewed a little differently, communion is also a symbol of that welcome table for the whole global family. God wants all people at the table. Therefore, the church, maybe more than any other organization, should do everything it can to enhance the total human experience. We are all walking upon the same mountain. We are all looking for the same table. The true vision of communion is that a global family will find a way to live and work together as children of God, respectful of one another, compassionate and hopeful for one another, and not only for human beings, but for the entire planet upon which the feast of God is spread. It's not enough to remember the crucified and resurrected Jesus during the eucharist. Not enough to feel good about fellow church members. There is a much bigger vision contained in bread and wine, nothing short of well-being for the entire planet, a communion with nothing less than the universe.

This great ritual of the church wherein ancient words have been repeated again and again—"This is my body. This is my blood"—especially enhances two essential spiritual feelings for the journey: the feeling of connection with God and with one another. Communion, therefore, brings us home because, after all, home is the place where we are with people who love us and whom we love; home is that place where we hold people inside our hearts with the deepest feelings of gratitude.

When the church gathers to share the eucharist, we are really gathering around the welcome table of God. The emphasis should not be communion as a "have to" or "must do" or even a "supposed to do." That misses the point entirely.

Nor is it like taking a precautionary medicine or vaccine. Furthermore, communion that emphasizes correctness, correctness of thought, of feeling, of procedure, also misses the point. Often I meet people who are concerned about their personal worthiness as they come to the table of God. They are burdened by shame or guilt, sometimes not over any one thing they have done, but they run a low-grade fever over their own unworthiness before God. I wish there were some way to eliminate all "worthiness theology" from the face of the earth. It oppresses the soul. It deadens the human spirit. It damages the sense of community that Christ is trying to create.

If there were a child, for example, who came to the dinner table every evening with a feeling of unworthiness, we would quickly say there is something dysfunctional about that family or something deeply wounded within that child. Unworthiness doesn't enhance the human experience. It makes no sense to me why unworthiness is perpetuated in the church as genuine religious feeling, and, for some, a necessary predisposition for receiving the presence of God. This makes no sense in light of the true essence of God, who wants to love us with unconditional zest and vitality and creativity. Some people may have a psychological need to feel unworthy, but I doubt seriously if it is God's need. Therefore, to come to the table of God is to come into an experience of connection with God and with one another.

I know it's been recounted again and again. Tacked up on the walls of old Sunday school rooms. The subject of preachers, poets, and artists. The story itself has become, almost, almost a religious cliché. "There was a man who had two sons…" Yes, it is the drama of the prodigal son, and even that word *prodigal* seems strangely old and dusty, given the fact that most of us never even use the word unless we're talking about this particular story of the prodigal son. Yet I love this story, but I love it not just because of the story, not just because it's in the Bible, not just because it comes up in the liturgy of the church; I love it because it rings so true with real human experience.

This story is about finding home, that welcome table of God's presence. It's about making your way back home. It's about sitting in the railway station with a ticket for your destination. Homeward bound. It's about there's no place like home. It's about somewhere over the rainbow. It's about home is where the heart is. It's about back home again in Indiana. It's about my old Kentucky home. It's about sweet home Alabama. It's about the stars shining bright deep in the heart of Texas. It's about keeping the home fires burning. It's about making my way back to you. It's about I'll be home for Christmas if only in my dreams. It's about home. Home. Home. The sweetness of going home.

But the home I'm talking about is that ultimate home we find in the presence of God, and that is exactly what communion or eucharist offers, a moment of home. The Christian life is about making the journey home. God is with me all the time— I know that and you know that too—but every now and then I find God and feel God and experience God, and that moment is like coming home; or every now and then I have that wonderful feeling of being at home within myself and that moment is like God. One way the apostle Paul spoke about Christ is that God sent Christ into the world to reconcile the world back to God; in other words, Christ is trying to bring us back home.

What we know is that we can be breathing with our lungs, have our hearts beating inside our chests, be able to work and walk and play as human beings, and still not be home. We can be in a marriage and not be home. We can have children and not be home. We can have a job and money in the bank and not be home. Because home is not about a physical place, it is about a spiritual plane upon which we live, and upon that plane what we feel is love and acceptance, worth and value, joy and thanksgiving. That's home. That's real home. And that's exactly what God is trying to give us.

But why this story of a father and a son and another son rings so true is that, well, it's that we know that home is hard to find. God is hard to find sometimes. The young son in this story misses home. He rebelled against the family, squandered the family resources, made all kinds of bad decisions, and experienced all kinds of degrading consequences. Some of you know firsthand what that is like. Some of you know what it's like to make not just little mistakes, but colossal mistakes. Some of us are *Wendy's* people—W-E-N-D-Y-'S—*Wendy's* people; we pull up to that fast-food window of life and say, "I would like an order of heartache, pain, and loneliness, and while you're at it, *supersize* it!" *Wendy's* people! Some of us know how to supersize our alienation in life. And some of us know what it's like to have kids who supersize their heartache. Alcohol. Drugs. Debts. Relationships. And if you're thinking that it could never happen to your kids, be careful, because there are a lot of good parents who have tried everything, and everything they tried, and everything they hoped, and everything they prayed for just didn't work.

The prodigal son is a story about a human being who supersized his tragic life. Yet even more to the point, this is a story about God, and the heart of the story is that the essence of God is welcome. God keeps the home fires burning and the porch light on. God keeps hoping and waiting, seeking and searching. And what God offers is not "I told you so." We may say that to each other, but not God. God doesn't say, "How dare you come back home?" God doesn't say, "You're not welcome here." God doesn't say, "You can't come in until you apologize." Because coming home, at least coming home to God, is not about being good enough, it's about being open enough to receive God's welcome and affirmation.

The Jesus I have come to know does not want to grind people down further and further into the dust of their own brokenness. My fear, of course, is that this is exactly the kind of Christianity many have received. Not unlike Suzanne and Brian and thousands just like them. The God I believe in is not the kind of God licking his chops just to catch me and judge me. The Christianity I believe so passionately is not about slamming the door in the faces of people; it's throwing the door wide open, and if that's not good enough, then taking the door off the hinges, and if that's not good enough, tearing down the wall to build a bigger door.

People are lost. But people are lost not because God is going to throw them into hell or because they haven't been good Christians or they haven't been morally good enough. They are lost in the same way I'm lost and you're lost; they have not found home. It's the home that is within us, that spiritual home of which I am thinking. That's the home we are all desperate to find.

It had been such a long journey for the prodigal son. But no matter how far he strayed, he never forgot the feeling, the hope, the possibility of home. He made his way back, and, interestingly enough, he came back with a feeling of unworthiness. Notice that unworthiness was his feeling. It's the very feeling the church has specialized in for two thousand years. Unworthiness. God help us when we think unworthiness is a religious feeling, and God help us even more when we think it is a religious requirement to find God. In this story, immediately, the feelings of his unworthiness were banished by his dad. Home is not about being worthy, it's about being welcomed. And so, the party ensues, the feast begins, the gifts are given. Why? Because that's how God feels when you and I come home. Maybe they had pizza and watched *The Tonight Show.*

Harold Kushner tells the old Jewish story about a sage who came home from the synagogue one day and found his nine-year-old daughter crying bitterly. He asked her what was wrong, and she told him between sobs that she and her friends had been playing hide-and-seek, and when it was her turn to hide, she hid so well that they had given up on finding her and went off to play another game. She waited and waited for them to find her, and finally after about an hour, she found herself all alone. He comforted his daughter, but eventually said, "My dear, I wonder if God ever feels like that, I wonder if God ever feels lonely?"[2]

Ah, the loneliness of God. The young man left the house and lost his home. The dad stayed in the house, but do you see, he lost his home too? The dad was just as lost without the son as the son was lost without the dad. We need God. But God needs us, because if God is love then love has to find some way, some how, some one to receive it. That's why the celebration was so rich and riotous. The son had come home and the dad had found home. And when you and I move our lives toward God, we find acceptance and love. That's good for us. But it's good for God because God is lonely in God's own bones until we finally come home.

One more twist on an old story. For years Garrison Keillor created that wonderful imaginary town of Lake Wobegon, Minnesota, where all the men are strong, the women good-looking, and the kids above average. In addition to telling his wonderful stories week after week, he also wrote a poem about Lake Wobegon, but it's also a poem about leaving home and coming home, and if you use your imagination, it's also a poem about coming home to God.

> One more spring in Minnesota,
> To come upon Lake Wobegon.
> Old town I smell your coffee.
> If I could see you one more time–
> I can't stay, you know, I left so long ago,
> I'm just a stranger with memories of people I knew here.
> We stand around, looking at the ground.
> You're the stories I've told for years and years.
> That yard, the tree–you climbed it once with me,
> And we talked of cities that we'd live in someday.
> I left, old friend, and now I'm back again.
> Please say you missed me since I went away.
>
> One more time that dance together,
> Just you and I now, don't be shy.
> This time I know I'd hear the music
> If I could hold you one more time.[3]

Living with faith in God is like coming home. It's like hearing the music of life, of love for the very first time. It's coming home to that table where love is present. When the prodigal son came home for dinner, there was a glorious celebration. Luke mentions that in the distance you could hear the music. All good welcome tables should have music. But there's a rumor, not in Luke's gospel and completely unsubstantiated, but a rumor that if you had been looking at that house from a distance, looking at it when that father and son embraced one another, that it looked a little bit like they were dancing. That's right, *One more time that dance together / Just you and I now, don't be shy / This time I know I'd hear the music / If I could hold you one more time.*

In all kinds of ways, in sanctuaries great and small, urban churches, country churches, Christians have taken bread and wine, remembering not just Jesus, but the love of God that broke open to the world through Jesus. And that bread and wine has constituted an invitation from the universe. God bids us to the welcome table. God invites us to come home to ourselves.

CHAPTER FIFTEEN

Mapping the Myths

The way that God gives and calls us to walk is the way of life and blessing, not death and curse. We are to carry the scriptures with us as we walk; and, with their help and the inspiration of the Holy Spirit, we are to wrestle with them in relation to the contexts, promises, and difficulties of our times.

CLARK M. WILLIAMSON[1]

"It all comes back to the Bible." That's what Suzanne told me when she finally came by my office to have a heart-to-heart talk about her faith. "It all comes back to the Bible."

Even as I sit down and write this chapter of the book, the tape of that unforgettable conversation begins to play with all the vividness of a dramatic movie. Suzanne called and asked for an appointment. Not surprisingly, she told me over the phone that she had some concerns about the church and wanted to talk about them. My immediate response was one of acceptance and welcome. I love it when people want to talk about the church. Yet underneath my words of welcome and

136

invitation, I could feel my heart begin to beat a little faster, the way it does when I feel conflict beginning to swirl in a relationship. I suspected she wanted to talk about what she perceived, at least, to be my lack of faith in the Bible as the Word of God. After she arrived at my office, my suspicions were confirmed. Even though it was a beautiful fall day outside, the leaves turning into their show-off brilliance of red and yellow and orange, I could feel a storm gathering inside my stomach.

After a few minutes of small talk—most people are extremely polite to the minister, not all, but most—she said, "I think I've figured out why I've been struggling with the church so much and with some of the things you've been preaching from the pulpit. You see, it all comes back to the Bible. You either believe the Bible is the literal Word of God or you don't. What I pick up is that you think the Bible is just another book. You think the Bible was written by men. That's why you're always interpreting it. Well, I don't believe in interpreting the Bible. It's okay to get background material, that's fine, but I believe the Bible is the revealed Word of God. I believe in the miracles. They're not just nice stories, but I think they really happened. I believe the Bible teaches that Jesus was God. I believe everything in the Bible, and I think what needs to happen is for our church to get more into the Word than what it does right now."

I must admit, even though I had my suspicions that this would be the conversation, I still didn't quite know where to start or how to respond after she shared her thoughts and feelings. I'm guessing there is hardly a mainline Protestant minister who hasn't had this conversation in his or her office with a church member. It's just another reflection of the theological fault line. A part of me wanted to be pastoral in my response, communicating to her that I understood her need to believe in this kind of biblical authority; that if she needed to view the Bible in this way, it was fine with me. I wanted to say something like, I might have a different viewpoint from you, but we shouldn't allow our views on the Bible to come between our humanity. Let's just live and let live.

Yet to be perfectly honest about what I was feeling at that moment, there was another response scaling the wall inside my gut. I wanted to respond with anger and impatience. I wanted to release some of my theological weariness and fatigue. I wanted to tell her that I'm dismayed at how thoughtful and intelligent people can view the Bible as a literal answer book dropped down from the sky by God. I wanted to rattle off passage after passage after passage in the Bible that present pictures of God that are nothing short of reprehensible. I wanted to point out that no one follows the Bible completely, that there's no way to read the Bible without interpreting the Bible. I wanted to share with her that people can understand the Bible inside-out but still miss the fundamental spirit of the Bible. There was a part of me, at least for a few seconds, that wanted to push back and be a theological bully. I didn't respond like that, but for a brief moment, I felt like that.

However, something quite wonderful started to happen in that office. I attempted to take the tension of the moment and dance with it until it was transformed into an opportunity. I said, "You know, Suzanne, I appreciate you coming by. I really do. There's a part of me that wants to convince you that you're wrong and I'm right. I suppose that's a very human response, and one that I'm not particularly proud of. But what I would really like to do is take some time and explain what I think the Bible is and what it is not, why I think the Bible is important in some ways and not so important in other ways, and more importantly, I would really like to help you understand why I love the Bible and why I think it can be a great resource for our Christian lives. You might agree. You might not agree. That's not the point. I just would like the chance to help you see there's another way, another *Christian* way of understanding the role of the Bible for our spiritual lives."

She said, "Well, I think I probably know what you're going to say, but I'm willing to listen."

"That's all I can ask," I said. "Let me tell you why I love the Bible and why I think it's so important to our spiritual lives."

And with that said, a conversation of incredible adventure began.

For those of you who have been reading this book all the way through, you've already discovered I prefer imagination over explanation. And for sure, I prefer poetry over exposition.

Therefore, I want to suggest an image that continues to make sense to me as I reflect upon the role of the Bible for the spiritual life, not only for the life of the church, but for the human quest to open the heart to God. It's the very image I shared with Suzanne.

I'm more and more convinced that the Bible is really a map for the heart. It's by no means the only map, but it is a map, a unique one for Christians. Our feelings and experiences are important. What we continue to learn from the arts and sciences is important. Insights from other cultures and religions are important. But the Bible, particularly for the church, the Bible can be an incredibly helpful map for opening the heart—not to achieve a system of right religion—but to read the Bible in such a way as to discover the rightness of opening the human heart to God. It's in the heart where divine energy lives, but the Bible, when read with an open heart, can facilitate that marvelous connection to heart energy.

A map is not a blueprint. When I think of a blueprint, I think of detailed, unalterable instructions that must be followed if the building is to turn out right. When it shows a measurement is twenty feet, that means it *must* be twenty feet, not twenty-one feet but twenty feet. There is no room for error or adjustment. You don't take a blueprint and go off freelancing. In many ways, every religious fundamentalist understands the Bible to be a blueprint.

Yet if religion is trying to come to terms with the mystery of that which is both beyond and within our experience, then there is no way a blueprint will work. It is, of course, possible to build two identical houses—that's what a blueprint can do; however, when it comes to shaping a human life, not only is it impossible to duplicate a spiritual life, it's not even desirable. Just as we know that every human being has a unique genetic code of DNA, so it is also true with our spiritual DNA. How we are moved by God, how we understand God, how we resonate with love and hope and gratitude in life cannot be prescribed in a blueprint. Not only does the heart not need a blueprint for the spiritual life, the heart resists such artificial attempts to draw artificial lines for the spirit.

Instead of a blueprint, what makes sense to me is that we understand the Bible as a map for the heart, mapping the large, mythic patterns of what it means to be on a spiritual journey. When I read the Bible stories of creation found in the book of Genesis, I'm not reading a blueprint for how to make a universe. I am, however, reading a map for what it means to understand what is at the heart of the universe, and in turn, what is at the heart of my heart–beauty and creativity and hope. When I read in the book of Exodus the story of Israel's liberation from Egypt, I'm not reading a blueprint of how this happened in a literal, historical, verbatim kind of way. Contrary to Cecil B. DeMille and Charlton Heston, what I hear is not a divine verbatim but the true voice of God, a voice for liberation in so many different ways, a voice against all kinds of oppression, including the oppression that lingers inside my human heart and Suzanne's heart. I even hear the voice of hope that calls every human being to the other side of drudgery and boredom and deadness, crossing over to the shores of life and celebration. And the same could be said of the stories that I read about the life of Jesus in the New Testament. Is there history in these stories? Yes, but how much is hard to tell, and at what point is even more difficult to tell, but beyond what is history and actual, there is the map that leads to something even more important than history, namely, the possibility of touching something real, something meaningfully, powerfully, spiritually real. The map of the Bible may not give us all the history we want, but it certainly gives us all the spiritual reality we can handle.

The Bible is a tremendous resource for faith, not because it begs to be followed like a blueprint, but because it gives us such rich material of how other men and women on the path of faith have tried to open their hearts to God. I read the Bible, listening to the experiences of others: Abraham and Sarah, Moses, Ruth and Job, Paul, Jesus, Mary and Martha. I listen to their experiences with one ear, but with my other ear I am listening to the beat of my own heart. Therefore, the Bible becomes a map of religious myth. The myths they were living and expressing, and the myths I am living and exploring, come together like an intricate symphony as I read the Bible. It's important to remember that a myth is something that is a larger pattern of reality that is eternally true within the human experience. Obviously, the Bible can't find God for me. Nor is finding the Bible the same as finding God. But when I read the Bible, fully aware that I am on my own spiritual pilgrimage, it has the remarkable power to swing open a little wider the doors of my heart. Perhaps a way of saying it is that the Bible provides heart maps for the journey.

Maps are indispensable when it comes to travel. As I mentioned earlier, not long ago my wife, Marti, and I were traveling in France. We rented a car and drove from Paris to Chartres, and then from Chartres down to the Loire Valley to the Chateau at Chenonceaux, and then from the Loire Valley we drove up to Brittany and stayed in the little town of St. Malo. It was a wonderful trip, but we could not have made it without a map. The map gave us a larger vision of what the trip was about, where we were going, the best way to get there, even a rough idea of how long it would take to get to where we wanted to go.

Nevertheless, there was much the map did *not* do for us. The map did not prepare us for that feeling of awe and mystery we experienced while walking the labyrinth at the Cathedral in Chartres. The map had no indication that while dining on the patio of the inn where we were staying in Chenonceaux, Le Bon Labourer, that we would have one of the best meals that has ever touched our lips, food so good I am determined to return to that place just to make sure it wasn't a dream. And the weather was perfect that evening. And the summer light lingered long into the evening. And we had this feeling that the day would never end. And the map did not say a colorful hot-air balloon would fly overhead while we relished our dinner, creating for us a sense of fascination and freedom, that whole evening becoming like fresh air for the soul. Furthermore, the map did not tell us that the inn where we had a reservation in St. Malo the next night would be perfectly awful. The kind of place that looked like it was straight out of an old Alfred Hitchcock movie. (I was convinced the woman keeping the inn was an axe murderer!) We only stayed one night instead of the scheduled two. We saw nothing about that on the map.

After we returned home from our trip, I don't think I ever said to anyone, "What a great time we had! Would you like to see our map? Let me show you what a lovely map we used. Oh

look, we took some pictures of our map; isn't it wonderful?"
Ridiculous? Of course. It's ridiculous because the point of
having the map was not to admire the map. The point of the
map was to help us get to the experiences we wanted to have–
and some we had not even imagined having–so that our hearts
could be rich with intensity and meaning. Filling the heart is
what it's all about.

I love the Bible. I really do. Early on in my graduate school
experience, I had decided I was going to be the next Rudolf
Bultmann, the greatest New Testament scholar in the twentieth
century. But as much as I love the Bible, it is not at the center
of my faith. It's only a map. Well loved. Well treasured. And
sadly, not read nearly enough by most people; but it's still only
a map. If I am to be a true follower of Jesus, not to mention if I
have learned anything from other world religions, then I have
to make sure God is at the center of my faith. I don't worship
the Bible because worshiping the Bible would be like taking
vacation pictures of a map. That's surely not the point of
vacation. I read the Bible because it helps me see how others
have searched and strained to open their hearts to God. I read
the book of Job, for example, and I too question where the
presence of God is in the world. I read the book of Jonah and
question what it is that I'm running from in my life. Am I
running from myself? From friendships? From intimacy with
my wife? From my responsibility as a minister? I read about
Jesus praying for release from his suffering in the garden, and I
think of the number of people I have been with while they
were dying, and I wonder why life has to be so hard, why
dying has to be so difficult, and I've also wondered, because I
think Jesus was feeling this, if life is really worth all the trouble.

These are heart maps of the human experience, and when
the Bible is read by the spiritual pilgrim, it begins to jump and
dance with relevance, not because it gives us all the answers,
but because it points us to well traveled trails. And yes, the
Bible can mean and should mean something a little different
to everyone who reads it because none of us are at the same
place on the journey. There are some pretty silly interpretations
out there, and frankly, some that I think are just plain wrong,
but having said that, part of the power of the Bible is its

inspirational ability to speak to the heart again and again. Not only again, but it can also speak anew to the heart.

Through the years I have preached several sermons on the Christmas story. Every Christmas Eve when the candles are lit at University Christian Church and the poinsettias have all been expertly arranged, the scripture text that is read is always the same, the gospel of Luke, chapter two, around twenty verses. Although the scripture reading may be the same, the sermons are always different. It's not because of my creativity, but because I am at a different place on the journey each year. And so is the church. And so is the world. What we need to hear year after year, or what we are even able to hear, changes. In other words, you read the part of the map you need at the moment. (While driving through France, I wasn't reading a map of Italy.) The Bible is inspired, not because it came down from a God-tube up in the sky, but because it has the power to meet us anew.

There are certain questions I find myself asking, therefore, as I read the inspiring stories of the Bible. Recognizing that the Bible is a compilation of books written by different men (and women?) across many different centuries, I begin asking questions like:

What was going on during that time?

What historical circumstances gave rise, not that dropped down, but gave rise to these words I'm reading?

Is there anything in my situation that might be similar? Usually there is. It's called the human experience. To follow Harold Bloom's thought, we need to read "humanly."

As I read the Bible, I try not to become too distracted by some of the reprehensible surface circumstances. Pillaging villages. Homophobia. Misogyny. Racism. Superstition. It's all found in the Bible because it was all found in the world that produced the Bible. Instead, I try to dive down a little deeper, asking about the larger patterns of myth and meaning, the real stuff of the heart; looking for the dynamics of religious experience that cross culture, that transcend time, that challenge even the twenty-first century; listening for the voice of the divine, that which comes from God's heart, as opposed to snagging my britches on the verbatim words of the text.

I try to figure out how it speaks to my heart and experience, my longings and vulnerabilities as a man. Sometimes reading the Bible is challenging to my life of faith. Sometimes it comforts my faith.

I assume there is always something in my heart that needs to be pried open by these ancient words, and so I find myself asking, What do I need to hear? How does it speak to me? What insight is there for me to experience? All pretty good questions when you think about it.

In a word, what I seek as I use the map of the Bible is *enlightenment* for the heart, and enlightenment is never finished. These were some of the thoughts I shared with Suzanne as we sat in my office and shared our thoughts and ideas. I'm not sure I really convinced her of anything, but I do think it helped her realize that there is another way of thinking about the Bible, a little broader, a little more realistic, and perhaps, perhaps just a little deeper. We do no favor to the Bible by trying to make it more than what it is or less than what it is. The key, it seems to me, is for people to find the courage and time to open it up, not because it has all the answers from God, but because we are desperate for some maps, maps older and wiser than ourselves, maps that can help us discover that we are not alone on the journey.

CHAPTER SIXTEEN

The Divine Dialogue

The best way to encourage someone to think is to ask questions and interact with the answers. That is the method of dialogue, and dialogue in its finest form involves just two people. Your answer to one question determines what the next question should be...If there is a renewal of thinking in the church, there will be church renewal. Without it, there won't. Trying to renew the church with gimmicks, or merely by arousing emotion, will not do the job. The church is strong only when it lives by the mature convictions of its members. Mature convictions are shaped in thought.

JOHN B. COBB, JR.[1]

It seems to me that when the church turns faith into an answer and not a question, an explanation and not an adventure, then the church is settling for far too little. The human experience propels us to ask questions of life, raising our doubts and expressing our deepest existential fears, but our humanity also has the capacity, even the desire, not to settle for shallow answers, premature answers, answers that may well be no

145

answers at all. There is a communion we all long for, a communion that is a relationship with the truth of God.

One of my biblical heroes is Thomas, the one who has been labeled Doubting Thomas. Found in the gospel of John, the story of Thomas demonstrates, not the recalcitrance of unbelief, but the courageous attempt to reach beyond easy answers and quick explanations when it comes to religious experience. The story develops around the personal experiences of some of the disciples who had discovered the risen Christ. They told their story enthusiastically to one another and found new inspiration in their encounter with the divine. But Thomas missed it. Jesus had been there, his friends had made this monumental discovery, but Thomas missed Jesus the way some of us miss a connecting flight at the airport. Therefore, he refused to believe.

What I find engaging is that his refusal to believe was actually a sign of belief. To believe means that we open ourselves to be seriously encountered by God, that we find God of utmost importance and are therefore willing to push and pull, excavate, struggle, and search to find that which is of ultimate value in our living. After years of teaching experience, I can attest to the fact that questions from students indicate interest and passion for the topic. It's sometimes said, "You can't know unless you ask." But it's also true, "You don't ask unless you care." To care about something with heart, mind, body, and soul is the essence of faith. Thomas, therefore, entered into the divine dialogue, the most powerful dialogue ever to be engaged.

I was at a religious service several years ago that pulled together a variety of clergypersons in response to a community tragedy. A mentally ill man had entered a church, shooting several young people before pulling the trigger and taking his own life. It was the kind of event that was devastating to the immediate families and the entire city of Fort Worth. However, the theological response I heard again and again from Christians was, "Our God is sovereign! Our God is sovereign!" I have grown to detest that expression, partly because I think it's a cliché, but partly because I think it betrays the fundamental essence of God and faith. Here was a disturbing tragedy, the kind of tragedy that has the power to rock all security in God, in church, in the world, and the only response that was given was a cliché suggesting God is in complete control. I think some questions would be in order after such a tragedy: some gut-wrenching, broken-hearted questions about how God works in the world, about how God answers or doesn't answer prayer, about what our community is and isn't doing about the safety of children, about how we can as a city allow a person to become so isolated, so mentally ill that we are susceptible to tragedies such as this shooting. These are the Thomas-like questions that express genuine faith. To say that God is sovereign says nothing. Let me soften that just slightly and offer this take on the expression "God is sovereign." I think what people may well have been trying to affirm is that there is something of God that endures both within and beyond the events of our lives. That I affirm and believe. I don't think that God controls events, but I do believe that God never abandons us nor forsakes us. However, saying God is faithful is not quite the same as saying God is completely sovereign.

Back to that growing chasm of faith in American culture. Some want to present a God, believe in a God who has all the answers, who is controlling every event that happens in the world, a God who is monolithic and unchanging, a God who works in the world in only one way, who can be understood in only one way, who can be defined as truth in only one way. To say that "Our God is sovereign!" completely shuts down any propensity toward authentic questioning and faithful curiosity. Doubts aren't allowed. Only acceptance. Explorations aren't allowed. Only conclusions. Grief isn't even allowed. Only obeisance. If God isn't really afraid of our doubts and questions—I don't think God is—then why are we so afraid of them? All of us might do well to pray the words of William Blake from time to time, "God save us from single vision."

I believe in synchronicity, and right in the middle of writing this chapter, this is not an exaggeration, a member of my congregation came by to say he was going through a period of wilderness. Part of the wilderness was personal. He had tragically lost a loved one several years ago and was still asking questions of God around that loss. His parents were divorcing, and he was reeling over how his parents could abandon their marriage and family after more than thirty years together. His questions were also theological, theological in the sense that he had lived most of his adult life with his childhood faith, and so he was asking questions about his faith, about the meaning of theological language and traditional Christian belief. In his words, "What in the world do I mean when I say that Jesus was the Son of God? What does it really mean to be a Christian? What does it mean that I am baptized?" Here was a man asking adult questions of God and of himself, and I found myself wanting to jump up and down in my office to applaud his journey. This kind of questioning is the larger hope I have for the church. Not that such journeys will be tolerated. Not that they will be permitted. But that journeys of this kind will be encouraged, indeed, become normative for the Christian experience. What my friend is after is the very same thing Paul Tillich called "the lost dimension of depth." That's the point of faith, to find the depth we are capable of experiencing as human beings; but I have no idea how a person can have depth without having dialogue with the deepest questions of life.

There is something life-giving and refreshing about seeing God as the great dialogue partner in life, as that one who helps us peel back the many layers of spiritual awareness. One way to process it is that God has many dimensions. There is that baseline dimension of God's existence. God is. Likewise, there is a part of human existence that deals with life at that baseline level of fact. I exist. Fact. I am working on a Dell laptop computer right now. Fact. It is true that the computer is plugged into the wall and running on electricity. Fact. It is true that I am sitting in a chair and listening to an old Joni Mitchell CD while writing this book. Fact. But life cannot be explained simply by the observance of simple facts. There is layer upon layer of meaning, and God is trying to bring each of us into a deeper dialogue with our human existence.

Beyond truth as fact, there is truth as authenticity. My daughter Katie is seventeen years old, and I love her very much. I am legally responsible for her. She has my genetic makeup (and her mother's!). We live in the same house together. All of that is truth at a certain level, but every now and then we have our moments, moments of such wonderful authenticity that we reach new levels in our relationship. She has been going through a difficult time, struggling to know herself, to understand some depression she has been experiencing, reaching to find her true self in the midst of many adolescent pressures. I admire her courage and struggle. But every now and then she shares something with me that is so deep, so real that, in fact, it feels like a new relationship because she is giving me the gift of her questions, and I am hearing them, hearing her at a new resonant level that is nothing less than human music. That is truth as authenticity. God the dialogue partner wants to move each of us deeper and deeper into a more authentic life. This is why, by the way, the Jewish prophets would often say to people, "Now, offering these sacrifices is fine and good, but what God really wants is a heart that is full of mercy and kindness and justice." That's truth at the level of authenticity. God is trying to move us closer and closer to the truth that is under the surface of the facts. This is why knowing the Bible is no guarantee of knowing God. Knowing a lot about God is not the same as knowing God. Knowing God is knowing God.

This kind of knowing requires an understanding that all truth, including the ultimate truth of God, has perspective. I cannot know anything outside of my own experience. It's just the nature of knowing. People cannot step out of their lives to know themselves, others, even God. I can only know God from within the limitations of my own experience. I look at a painting by Picasso, for example, as I did not long ago in Paris, and I realize that I cannot know that painting as a mere object. I cannot know what Picasso intended or was trying to say. I can only see the painting from my human perspective. It's the dialogue of truth. Some Christians who argue, for instance, that the Bible is the literal word of God and without any error whatsoever fail to appreciate the fact that even if the Bible were without error, neither they nor anyone else could be guaranteed to read it in errorless fashion. It just can't be done. Nor should it be done. God isn't trying to bypass people in order to pour some kind of religious truth into our brains as if we had removable garbage can lids on top of our heads. The bigger the truth, the greater the chances for perspective. This is why I suggested earlier that God isn't just the peak of the mountain, God *is* the mountain.

Additionally, dialogue with God moves us into the mystery of truth. I have a physical body, and a doctor might tell me I have a disease or a wound or something that needs to be treated. That is true. But there is another truth, the truth of how I feel emotionally. The truth of how I feel spiritually. The truth that is my mind and heart, not just the functioning of my brain, but the reality that is deeper than the physical tissue and chemicals in my brain. This is why I have been with people in their dying, even my own mother as I mentioned earlier in the book, and though their physiology was shutting down, their humanity was glowing with wholeness and aliveness. How can this be except that a deeper dialogue with truth is happening beyond physical explanation? Religion is about mystery, and mystery beckons dialogue.

Several years ago I was browsing through a little used bookstore in Indianapolis. To call it a store is probably being too generous. It was a little shack in a lousy part of town, built just a few yards away from an Interstate 65 overpass. It was tiny and crammed with books and old magazines and smelled pretty much like a high school gym locker. My kind of place. I would stop there from time to time because every now and then I would find one of those little treasures poking its head out from the shelf like a squirrel. If you're a book lover, you know exactly what I'm talking about.

I paid two dollars for the greatest treasure I ever found at that little bookstore. It's a book entitled *Adventures of the Mind*.[2] It was published in 1959. Isn't that a great title? *Adventures of the Mind*. It's a book of essays, all of which had been previously published in *The Saturday Evening Post*. These essays received wide circulation. And you need to understand something, this was no *People Magazine* or *TV Guide*. These were serious essays written by some of the best minds of the 1950s and 1960s. There's a chapter by Loren Eisley entitled *An Evolutionist Looks at Modern Man*. Another chapter was written by J. Robert Oppenheimer entitled *The Mystery of Matter*. Aldous Huxley, Arthur Schlesinger, Edith Hamilton all wrote chapters for this book. There's a wonderful essay in it that I've read again and again by Aaron Copland titled "The Pleasures of Music." It's delightful. And there was one theologian, Paul Tillich, who contributed a chapter, an essay entitled "The Lost Dimension of Religion."

I mention the book because I love what it symbolizes. *Adventures of the Mind.* That is, the mind going forth. The mind expanding. The mind becoming larger and larger. I love it because I believe that each of us has a religious mind. We have a religious capacity and aptitude. It's part of what makes us human beings. The great cathedrals of the world came from the religious mind. Some of the greatest artwork in the world came from the religious mind. The same could be said for music and poetry and literature; they all came from the religious mind. Jesus expanded the religious mind. He helped people understand God in a new way, God as love, God as compassion, God as wounded for the well-being of humanity. In fact, I think a case can be made that Jesus himself had a religious mind, and his religious mind expanded in extraordinary and remarkable ways. He was never the same after forty days in the wilderness. He was never the same after that life-threatening storm upon the Sea of Galilee. He was never the same after Mary and Martha and Lazarus. He was never the same after that agonizing betrayal in the garden. And yet, Jesus kept opening, expanding, deepening his religious mind before God.

Think about it like this...We are two-hump creatures. I know some camels have one hump, and some camels have two humps, but we are two-hump creatures as human beings. One hump is our capacity to live in the material reality of the world. Eating. Drinking. Working. Building. That's the material world. And we all have to live in that world. We have to buy insurance. We have to save for retirement. We have to change the oil in the car. We have to do laundry and clean the house. That's part of the material world. And there's nothing wrong with the material world. It's even true that we share biological instincts with other animals.

But there is another hump, if you will, that we carry. It's what I would call the religious mind. It's that human capacity to think beyond the material world of what we see or touch or hear. It's that ability to feel love, to long for hope, to touch the mystery of life at the deepest of levels. It is that capacity, even longing, to know that our lives mean something. Not that we just experience something, not that we just skim the surface of life like a water bug crawling over the pond, not that we just go through the biological motions of living, but that we find while living upon what Carl Sagan called "a mote of dust suspended in a sunbeam" that our lives mean something. And that means we connect our lives to a larger structure of the universe: that structure we often call G–O–D. We call it God. The vastness of God that is beyond us and the vastness of God that is within us. It's that God hump that makes us human.

What do we do with the religious mind? Well, it's a choice. It's a very human choice. It's your choice. It's my choice. Some people don't do anything with it, and, from my perspective at least, they live flat, material lives. Consuming the world day after day. Working day after day. Never really engaging in the big dialogue of life. What do we do with the religious mind? Some people keep the religious mind just a certain size. Oftentimes extra-small. The religious mind they developed about the time they were in kindergarten is the religious mind they live with throughout the complexity of their adulthood. What do we do with the religious mind? Some people nurture it for a season in life. They go through, as one person described it to me several years ago, "a religious phase." But where is the adventure of the mind? Where is the expansion of the religious mind? Where is the journey of the mind of faith?

A few months ago I rented the movie *Billy Elliot*. It's an inspiring story about a young boy, but more than that, it is an inspiring story of what it means to live the adventure of the mind. Billy Elliot was an eleven-year-old boy growing up in the bleak, depressing town of Durham, England. A working-class, industrial town. His mother had died. His father was a coal miner. And his father also drank too much. The father was hurt and wounded and bitter. He was trying to survive in the material world. But like any self-respecting dad, he made sure Billy went to the gym to learn boxing and wrestling. That might be fine for most boys, but not for Billy Elliot.

You see, Billy Elliot wanted to dance. He saw the girls taking ballet lessons, and he wanted to learn ballet. He would dance through the streets on his way home from school. He would dance in his room. It's not so much that he wanted to *be* a dancer as he *was* a dancer, a dancer in the deepest place of his soul. But his father could not imagine it. His world was too small. His view was too narrow. His perspective too limited. And so, Billy does the only thing he can do, he sneaks behind his father's back, and he learns to dance. Oh, he can dance. He's a prodigy. A brilliant prodigy. His father finds out about Billy's lessons and beats him. Curses him. Says to him, "Lads do football or boxing or wrestling, not ballet!" In a way, the whole movie is about Billy Elliot trying to break out of his dad's small world, so he can know for himself the larger world of dance and art, so he can know the expansion of his own mind.

True religious experience is a dialogue with the depth and breadth, the length and height of God's love. That is to say, the Holy Spirit is always trying to expand the religious mind. The Holy Spirit doesn't want to make our religious minds smaller; the Spirit wants the mind to venture forth; the Spirit wants us to understand how really vast God is; the Spirit wants us to see that at the heart of faith is the comprehensible/ incomprehensible love of God. This is the very reason why Christians and religious people all over the world take time to worship. We worship because the religious mind is in awe, is struck, is reverent, is overjoyed by the greatness of the divine. That's why we have faith, and that's why believing in God and explaining God are not the same thing. Faith is first and foremost opening our hearts to the yawning vastness of God. I guess that's why I love that book and the title of that book I found years ago, *Adventures of the Mind.* I love it because I think God calls us to be on that spiritual adventure, and there is no adventure without understanding God as the dialogue.

Billy Elliot did escape his dad's small world, his brother's small world, his town's small world. He didn't do it, however, all on his own. He had a few people, a teacher, a friend or two, who saw something in him, saw something bigger and more meaningful for him. And they helped him. Billy Elliot became a member of the Royal Academy of Ballet in London. He found a bigger world because he could imagine it. The movie ends, no surprise, with Billy dancing in the wonderful ballet *Swan Lake*. And to top it all off, his dad and brother are present cheering in the crowd. No longer the little skinny kid from Durham, he is now the handsome, athletic young man taking center stage. Billy Elliot has become beautiful.

There is nothing more beautiful than when the Spirit of God helps us imagine the depth and breadth, the length and height of both the mystery of human life and the mystery of God. It is the adventure of the mind, and it is what it means to be alive. Moreover, it's what it means to be a disciple of Jesus. The day we stop asking, "What is the meaning of my life?" is the day we settle for too small a world. Paul Tillich has written about it in this way: "Being religious is the state of being concerned about one's own being…It means asking passionately the questions of the meaning of our existence and being willing to receive answers…It is the search for our lost dimension of depth." Pretty good words from a book found years ago in a dusty shack of a bookstore. Pretty good words for what it means to live, not with a fortresslike God, but with a God who is open and ready to receive our questions, a God who beckons us to live the adventure of the religious mind.

CHAPTER SEVENTEEN

The Crucible of the Church

When I was at the end of my rope, the people at St. Andrew tied a knot in it for me and helped me hold on. The church became my home in the old meaning of "home"—that it's where, when you show up, they have to let you in. They let me in.

ANNE LAMOTT[1]

People are riding their bikes through Trinity Park in Fort Worth, Texas. It is hot, but not nearly as hot as it will be later in the day. Mothers are pushing strollers with little babies cooing and clapping their hands. They are enjoying the fresh morning air. Teenagers are shooting a basketball on the court next to Tanglewood Elementary School. Couples are walking together. Some moving at a leisurely pace, holding hands and talking. Still others are moving along at power-walk pace, revving up their cardiovascular systems and breaking into a healthy sweat. Across the street at Yogi's Café there is a frenetic quality of aliveness in the air. Coffee. Bagels. Fresh fruit. Omelettes. People are eating, reading newspapers, sitting and talking to one

155

another in their shorts and tennis shoes, T-shirts and sport shirts.

Is it just another morning?

Not exactly.

It's just another *Sunday* morning in Fort Worth, Texas.

The disconnection between American culture and the Sunday morning church experience has never been greater than it is right now. Never. It is by now well documented that American culture, not just individuals, but the culture itself supported the institutional presence of the mainline church for past generations. The reasons for that support have not always been noble or carefully reasoned in any theological sense. Regardless, there was a connection, a kind of internal structure that ran from cultural consciousness to the church community. People went to church. Supported the church. And even those who didn't go to church still considered the church an important institution for individuals and society. Ministers in churches were respected leaders. Activities in churches were respected.

The how and why of church participation is as elusive as chasing cottonwood fluff through the air. In more theologically conservative churches, members are often made to feel guilty if they do not participate and attend their churches. Guilt and shame can go a long way in building participation, but it runs counter to everything the gospel is about. If the gospel of Christ is about God's gracious invitation to love and life, shame and guilt should have no part in the church equation. On the other hand, I'm afraid more liberal churches have confused God's grace with indifference and apathy. Therefore, if shame is out of the picture and if guilt is out of the picture, why should people participate in a church community, especially one associated with mainline Protestantism?

Churches have existed because in one way or another they believed they had the truth. Not just any truth, but God's truth, the truth of the Christian gospel that through Jesus Christ all people who stand before God can be forgiven and saved and not merely saved in some personal sense, but in a cosmic sense, in the sense that faith was and is a life or death matter. Obviously, some churches hold this truth more dogmatically than others, but truth has always been the driving force of the church, even the mainline Protestant church.

It is apparent that the overall appreciation for institutional life in American culture has been in a serious decline for decades. Part of this can be rooted in an overall suspicion of institutions, particularly post-Vietnam and post-Watergate. Part of this can be understood as an increase in American individualism, rooted as much in personal consumerism as anything. How we arrived here is not nearly as important as understanding where here is, and here is a culture that basically thinks religious truth and value, spiritual thought and feeling, indeed even God, can be found outside the parameters of the institutional church. It is the decentralization of God. This is the reason why the mantra of the early twenty-first century has become, "I'm very spiritual but not very religious." That is, people feel as if they can find God on their own and don't need the baggage or the commitment to the institutional life of a church.

This is a major shift. At one time people had to go to church in order to find the truth because the church was the gatekeeper of the truth. The church possessed the message, the magic, the sacred so desperately needed in human experience. The church possessed the myths around which people could organize their lives. Creation. Redemption. Even myths that promised a certain eternal assurance and future. For the most part, these old religious myths no longer have the compelling force they once enjoyed. The "death of God" theology several years ago was in fact wrongly named. It was not the death of God that was shaking the church to the foundations, but the death of myths, old ways of speaking about reality that no longer ring true for our society. We now live in a culture in which the gates to truth have been torn down; therefore, if there are no gates, why have the gatekeepers? In other words: Why church?

I want to suggest that the church has to come to grips with the fact that we don't have the capital T truth. In fact, we have something much more precious than truth, we have *truthfulness*. We have a message about God's love in Christ, an opening to the divine, a presence of God that still has the power to create lasting personal and global transformation. We have a religious perspective grounded in the story of Jesus, and this perspective can create a lively engagement with humanity, making a positive difference in the human search for authenticity and truth, making a positive difference in the spiritual search for God. The Christian faith offers a compelling outlook on life and faith, it provides some answers and insights, all of which I personally treasure, but even more, the Christian faith can invigorate and guide the human search for ultimate meaning. What we offer to the world is not a conclusion, but a journey. An exploration, not an explanation. An adventure of faith and an experience of faith. The point of the Christian faith is not to believe in the Christian faith (a point even ministers and theologians are prone to forget). The point of faith is to encounter the living presence of God at the deepest levels of human experience.

Yet I would contend there is an inextricable connection between being part of a church community and discovering the truthfulness of God. From my perspective, church communities become crucibles of spiritual formation and transformation. (Thinking of other world religions, I think the same case could be made. Jewish communities enhance the Jewish experience. Buddhist communities enhance the Buddhist experience, and so forth.) One way to think about it is this: In our contemporary culture, very few people need to be convinced of the spiritual significance of Jesus or even the importance of nurturing the religious dimension of life. The cutting-edge apologetic now seems to be helping people understand the importance of belonging and participating in the Jesus/Spirit community. Part of the mission of the church is to call people to a religious adventure, an adventure that radically includes participation within a faith community.

The metaphor of the church as the *body of Christ* is significant because just as the physical body is essential for a full human experience, so also is a community essential for a full spiritual experience. A compelling case can be made, both in message and practice, that part of the spiritual journey will never blossom unless it is rooted in community. This makes fellowship with others compelling, worship in corporate settings essential, service to the world joined hand-in-hand with others special, learning with others and from others of paramount importance. This is not the same as denominational support and institutional loyalty. Nor is it a way of saying that people of faith are ready to get behind a bureaucratic church program. It is, however, a way of linking the spiritual life to the concrete experience of congregational interaction with other people. Part of the interpretive edge of the gospel today has to be the invitation not only to experience God's grace, but also to join God's gracious community. Not because the community is the sole possessor of truth—an old paradigm from another generation—or that the church community can exercise some kind of coercive authority over the lives of people—an even older paradigm of the church—but because at a soulful level spiritual truthfulness is found within the crucible of community.

If the church community is not a place of authoritarian truth but experiential truthfulness, it stands to reason that the church must become a place of radical conversation. Conversation means exploration, questions and answers, more questions, the process of being able to probe the longings of the spirit within the parameters of scripture and the traditions of the church. Conversation and community are rooted in the gospel; that is to say, this isn't a mere cultural adjustment on the part of a declining mainline church, but is part and parcel of what it means for a congregation to be a congregation. The gospel, for that matter religion itself, is about binding God and humanity back together. This is exactly what conversation does; true conversation brings people together. It creates mutual respect. Genuine sharing. Mutual benefit. To think of the gospel as opening up the deepest religious dialogue is not only intrinsically appropriate to the gospel, it is also thrilling as it invites the church to engage culture and people. Community, too, is intrinsic to the gospel. The very concept of the trinity, one of the more obtuse doctrines of the church, suggests that at the very heart of God's existence is a communal nexus. One cannot find God without finding community, because community is at the heart of God.

In my opinion, there is no one writing today who makes a better case for the church vis-à-vis spiritual experience than Anne Lamott. In her book *Traveling Mercies* she tells story after story, real human stories of how church community has shaped her spiritual life. For example, she tells the story of Ken Nelson.

Ken Nelson was a young man dying of AIDS. Kenny wandered into the church and became a regular attender. Although very ill, he participated in community, enriched the lives of others even as he was being nurtured by a church family. People looked out for Kenny, prayed for Kenny, and when he was not in church, it was like a hole punched through the Styrofoam cup of that congregation. But there was one particular Sunday when the congregation was singing the song "Jacob's Ladder." A wonderful old song I still remember from my childhood. Everyone was standing and singing, enjoying the opening hymn, everyone was standing except Kenny, because he was too tired, too weak, too physically ravaged to stand for the hymn.

While all this was going on there was a woman in the choir by the name of Ranola. Lamott describes her as "large and beautiful and jovial and black and as devout as can be." But Ranola, as can happen in a church community, had been standoffish and distant from Kenny. Who knows why? Who knows why humanity breaks down? But something changed that day, and it happened during the song, during the service of the church, happened in the midst of ordinary people opening themselves up to the extraordinary presence of God. Ranola looked at Kenny and then, as Lamott tells it, "her face began to melt and contort like his, and she went to his side and bent down to lift him up—lifted up this white rag doll, this scarecrow. She held him next to her, draped over and against her like a child while they sang. And it pierced me."[2]

And so it should pierce all of us.

There is truth, the kind that is explained and argued and reasoned, and then there is truthfulness, the kind that is experienced when people dare to be a church community. In the end, what makes us Christians (and better human beings) is not what we know but how we love. I think of the number of times I have worked with church members over the issue of AIDS. Their understandings of the gay community. (These two are not the same issue, of course, but they often force the church to reflect upon what it means to be an inclusive and welcoming community.) I have helped people explore these issues biblically and theologically. The discussions have been good and important. But the discussions all melt away when you see a woman by the name of Ranola pick up a man by the name of Kenny, holding him like a baby, holding him the way, well, surely the way God might like to hold all of us.

In Ignazio Silone's book *Bread and Wine,* the priest says, "If we live like him, it will be as if he never died."[3] And that is the genius of the church, a community of people willing to organize their lives around the life and presence of Jesus, recognizing there is a part of Jesus that we will only find when we are willing to look into the eyes of another.

Like Anne Lamott, Nora Gallagher tells about her remarkable spiritual odyssey with a faith community in the book *Things Seen and Unseen.* She recounts her relationship with a little Episcopal congregation in Santa Barbara, California. There she encountered the people of the parish, and there she encountered God. I find it striking that she makes discoveries about both community and herself while in the church, suggesting they are in essence the yin and yang of the same reality.

Two statements from Gallagher. She writes, "I learned about community: that being faithful to God means being faithful to others, in sickness and in health, for better, for worse." And again, "I came to this church five years ago as a tourist and ended up a pilgrim."[4]

My sense of our culture, generally speaking, is that a lot of people have become religious tourists, interested in picking this spiritual insight or that spiritual thought from the mix of religion, but when it comes to making a real commitment to community, that seems more and more in short supply. Yet there really is something to this experience of community. To participate in a community does not mean a person has to be small-minded and provincial. Nor does it have to be an experience of exclusivity. The church no longer can posture itself in the world as the sole carrier of the truth; in the end that is nothing but arrogant and damaging, but the church can and should offer the great spiritual invitation, offering to people the many different ways a church community can be a place where spiritual life is formed, where self-understanding can be found, where transcendent presence can be touched, and where service to the world can move forward.

I have to be honest here and say that not everything in the church is wonderfully healing and beautifully redeeming. As a minister, I have seen it all, the good, the bad, the ugly, even the appalling. (I'm guessing there may be someone reading this book who has been deeply hurt by the church or another form of organized religion. I meet people all the time who are recovering from church!) There is something glorious about being in community with one another, but there is a shadow side to community. Churches can be exclusive, hurtful, and petty. Churches can be bigoted, flawed, and frail. I have seen people leave the church over something as insignificant as the color of the new carpet or over one particular line from one particular sermon delivered on one particular Sunday morning. And beyond the congregational struggles, there are always the larger atrocities perpetrated by the church toward Jews and women and people of different faiths, and all of it, every last drop of it, is regrettable and indefensible.

Yet even within the struggles of community, there is wisdom to be gained and insight to be learned. I recently was engaged in a painful conversation with a leader from my church. He is a good man. But because of differences in outlook and perspective, there had grown between us a nagging distance. After a while, distance became conflict, and soon conflict became a clash of personalities and ideas. He said and did some hurtful things. I personalized his actions too much. To say the least, community had been broken between the two of us. But not long ago we sat down together, and what ensued was a difficult conversation. He told me about his concerns and hurts, not just one thing but many things about me and the church. There was a part of me that wanted just to listen, absorb it, and make a quick peace of it so we could get on with life. But I didn't. I told him of my hurt and anger and how what he had done and said damaged our relationship. I could feel myself shaking on the inside as I sat in a chair looking over at this man. I needed to be honest with him, but I wasn't sure if honesty would heal or explode our relationship. Could I really trust the inner meaning of church? We talked more. And more. Two hours later we reached a new place of understanding. He apologized. I apologized. In truth, we forgave each other and imparted the precious gift of a new start.

We did this partly because we wanted to, but partly because we both felt the claim of the church upon our lives. I am part of him and he is part of me. If I can't learn to treat him in a way that is consistent with the spirit of Christ, and if he can't learn to treat me similarly, then what is Christ energy all about? We don't have to come together at the point of rightness or agreement. The paradigm of rightness splits churches and families all the time. It's not truth that holds us together, but our willingness to risk this venture into truthfulness, the same kind of truthfulness that emanated from the life of Jesus.

Whether it's healing or helping, learning, growing, or stretching, religious community is part of spiritual formation. Relationships with others help us understand our relationship with God, and our relationship with God radically shapes our understanding of others. Henri Nouwen has written, "Dare to love and to be a real friend. The love you give and receive is a reality that will lead you closer and closer to God as well as to those whom God has given you to love."[5] There is a gifted quality to being in community. Not easy at times. Challenging at times. But also incredibly rewarding and inspiring at times. It is the gift of community. And it's the only good reason I can think of to interrupt someone reading *The New York Times* at Yogi's on a Sunday morning, inviting them to find themselves and their faith within a worshiping community of faith.

CHAPTER EIGHTEEN

Resources of the Spirit

If the Fire has come down into the heart of the world it is,
in the last resort, to lay hold on me and to absorb me.
Henceforth I cannot be content simply to contemplate it or,
by my steadfast faith, to intensify its ardency more and more
in the world around me...So my God, I prostrate myself
before your presence in the universe which has now become
living flame: beneath the lineaments of all that I shall
encounter this day, all that happens to me, all that I
achieve, it is you I desire, you I await.

PIERRE TEILHARD DE CHARDIN[1]

There is not a more thrilling story in the Bible than that of
the story of the day of Pentecost. Found in the book of Acts, it
represents the birthday of the church and the inauguration of
the Christian movement. As the story is told, the disciples
gathered in Jerusalem for a great Jewish festival and the Holy
Spirit came to them like a mighty rushing wind, a symbolic
suggestion, I think, that the Spirit of God is always trying to
come into our lives, touching us, moving us, inspiring us. I
love the part about the house shaking and the roof quivering

and the windows vibrating, a statement that the power of God is not some ordinary power, but it has the power to shake us down and help us see what is really important in life. I love the part about tongues of fire resting over the heads of the disciples, licking the sky with a kind of divine wildness, reminding us that the working of God cannot be contained nor controlled, but God works in the world like a dancing flame, that God wants to ignite something inside our lives. I love the part when they spoke in different languages, maybe it was mystical or ecstatic, I don't really know, all I know is that there were enough cultural differences that day to keep everyone separated and isolated from one another, but the Spirit of God broke down walls, broke down barriers, broke down partitions so that a new human community could be born.

One thing is for sure, each of us needs a spiritual resource, a spiritual reservoir inside our lives, and in Christian theology this resource is named the Holy Spirit. In John 7:38, Jesus says, quoting scripture, "'Out of the believer's heart shall flow rivers of living water.'" The verse continues, "Now he said this about the Spirit, which believers in him were to receive." There are, of course, churches that put a great deal of emphasis on the Spirit, to the point that some of them are called Pentecostal churches or charismatic churches. One of the hallmark characteristics of these congregations, beyond the fact that they tend to literalize the Bible and the Christian faith, is a passionate belief that the primary identifiable sign of having God's spirit is speaking in tongues, that wild and ecstatic experience in which people speak a different language or religious utterance. In mainline-type churches, the Holy Spirit barely receives a nod. This is partly due to an emphasis upon the intellectual dimension of faith, a dimension I completely support, but there is also a fear in talking about the Spirit, opening the heart and mind and soul to the mystery of the Holy Spirit of God. This fear is completely unnecessary, given the fact that the Spirit is associated with many dimensions of the Christian faith, none of which undermine the intellectual dimension of belief. I suppose I love the Pentecost story so much because I know that all of us, myself included, are desperate for this spiritual resource for life.

What does the Holy Spirit do inside the hearts of women and men? One way to answer that question is to appeal to a variety of metaphors associated with the Spirit, not the least of which is this metaphor of bringing people together in community. This happens because the Spirit's work is to create spiritual breadth and depth within the human experience.

I've been thinking a lot about a little phrase someone shared with me at a conference not long ago. The woman who shared it with me lives in rural Mississippi. She is African American. She has worked most of her life fighting the forces of racism and poverty. She is a mother. A grandmother. She is an activist and a poet and a folk artist. And one thing she told me about folk artists is that they would use whatever materials were available in order to create their craft. They might use corn husks or driftwood or buttermilk and berry dye to make paint. Folk artists create beauty because the Spirit of God moves them to create beauty, but to do it they have to use the materials at hand. And so she gave me a phrase that is becoming more and more my mantra, my little prayer to live by each day. The expression: *Use what you have to make what you need.*

The disciples were gathered together in a little house in Jerusalem on that first Pentecost. Had you told them by the end of the day they would have to accommodate the needs of three thousand people who would respond to the gospel, they would have been overwhelmed. Had you told them they would eventually spread the story of Jesus around the world, they would have been paralyzed with fear and overwhelmed with inadequacy. But the place to start is at the beginning, and the place to begin is at the start. The Spirit of God will work, sometimes beyond our wildest imagination, but we have to give the Spirit of God something to work with, provide the raw materials of a beginning place. It's a matter of using what you have to make what you need.

Not long ago there was an article in the *Houston Chronicle* about Itzhak Perlman. It was about a time when the great violinist was giving a concert at Avery Fisher Hall in New York City. It's an unforgettable sight to see Perlman take the stage. He was stricken with polio as a child, and so he has braces on both legs and walks with two crutches. He walks painfully, but also with an air of dignity and pride as he takes his place with the orchestra.

This particular night he was at the very beginning of the concert, having played only for a minute or so when something went wrong. Everyone in the audience could hear a loud snap, and there was no mistaking what the sound was, it was the breaking of a string. Everyone knew the concert had to stop. That the string would have to be replaced. Everyone knew that he would have to slowly, painfully walk offstage, replace the string, slowly, painfully walk back onstage. Then and only then could the music continue.

But that's not what happened that night. Perlman waited for a few seconds, closed his eyes, signaled the conductor, and the orchestra began to play. He played with overwhelming power and purity and passion. You're not supposed to be able to play a symphonic work with only three strings, but he did. He was able to take what he had and make the music he could make, even making new and inspiring sounds from that instrument. How is it that this musician, who trained his entire life to make music with four strings, could make music with three strings, music even more memorable, more sacred, more beautiful than ever before, how could that happen? I think it's one of the cardinal principles of the Spirit. Use what you have to make what you need.

All of us at one time or another get caught in that trap of wishing life were different. (If only we would *work at life* as much as we *wished in life!*) If only I had more money...If only my kids were different...If only my health were better...If only the church had a better minister...If only more people were less apathetic...If only there were less poverty, less racism, less prejudice, less hatred...If only my house were nicer...If only there were more good men out there...If only there were more good women out there...If only I had more education...If only more people participated in our community...If only the economy were better...If only the public schools were better...If only America were better...If only the world were better...If only God were better...And here's one, if only I had a dollar for every time I have thought or said that expression *if only* about my life, my church, my world.

God doesn't ask us to do what we can't or to become what we can't. God doesn't ask us to say what we can't or to have what we can't. But God does ask us to use what we have to make what we need. That's the genius of what happened on that day when the Spirit came and brought people together because they were courageous enough to be together in the first place. One way to understand the Spirit is to open the heart to building community and relationships with others.

Yet beyond the metaphor of building community, the Spirit also increases our religious imagination and enhances our ability to love one another, the obvious fact being there is no human community without love. One way to think about it is that there is an empty cup, an empty chalice inside each of our hearts and that chalice waits to be filled, even longs to be filled with the experience of love. We want to be loved. We want to know that we matter in this world. We want to know that we are significant in the eyes of the universe. But not only that, we want to love. We want to have that feeling of giving ourselves to something because when we love, we feel alive, not just close to another person, but we begin to feel close to God. And even when love brings us pain, and it does, it always does, we endure it and wade through it like a swamp because the rewards of love far outweigh the pain love might bring us.

It is the energy of love I sense while reading the book of Romans. Paul writes, "God's love has been poured into our hearts through the Holy Spirit that has been given to us." That is to say, the work of the Holy Spirit, living in that deepest place, in that most intimate place of our lives, is to pour divine love into our hearts. Not once. But again and again and again. Assuring us that we are loved by God. Assuring us that as we walk upon this planet we are not alone in the universe. Assuring us that in spite of failures and fear and frailty, we are held by a divine love. Yes, it is that Spirit who pours love into the chalice of our hearts. There is no more powerful religious experience than when, in the quietness of our own souls, we know ourselves as people who are beloved of God.

Maybe I like the pouring image so much because it suggests a kind of communion. Every now and then when it's quiet on a Sunday morning during one of our worship services at

University Christian Church, I can hear the wine being poured from the pitcher into the chalice during the celebration of the eucharist. A slight gurgling sound slips through the microphone. It's the sweet sound of pouring. I love seeing it and love hearing it because that one little gesture of pouring suggests that God poured God's very life energy out into the world for humanity. That God didn't hold back. That God didn't play it safe. That God didn't calculate the risk. Instead, so willing was Jesus to offer the invitation of God's love that he poured himself out, even to the point of dying on a cross. Therefore the cross, at one time a symbol of scandal, actually became a symbol of love, the kind of love that can still shake the human heart like a can of paint at the hardware store. It's that kind of love that is poured out into our hearts by the Spirit, and I dare say it is significant because we cannot love until we know and trust that we are loved. The Spirit of God assures us in most anxiety-ridden moments that we are loved by the divine. With that love poured into our hearts, we then find the courage we need to love others, those we know, those we don't know, those who are similar, those who are different; we love because love has been poured into our hearts.

And just as I mentioned earlier about the imagination of compassion, so also love requires imagination. One of the Spirit's trajectories for our lives is not to keep us the same, but to move us into a larger and larger religious consciousness. This becomes the work of the Spirit. As Paul has written, "The Holy Spirit strengthens our inner spirit." And again, he writes about how the Spirit inspires us to comprehend "what is the breadth and length and height and depth, and to know the love of Christ that surpasses knowledge." This is why true spiritual vitality is measured, not by what we know or by what we can explain, but by how much and how passionately we love. For Christians, this represents the essence of Jesus, and in turn, the essence of God. After all, at his most vulnerable moment in life, Jesus had a last supper with his disciples, and he punctuated it by draping a towel around his shoulders and, with a basin of water in his hands, proceeded to bend down and wash the disciples' feet one by one. His summary word was simple and replete with spiritual insight. He said, "Love one another as I have loved you." There is a place for the fulfillment of the self and personal success, but there is a part of the self that will never be fulfilled until we give it away.

There is one more metaphor of the Spirit I find fascinating. It verges on the mystical, but in truth, all religion is mystical. It is the work of the Spirit that brings us guidance and direction, even in our moments when we are most confused and lost. Have you ever been in a situation wherein you just didn't know which way to go? Have you ever reached a moment in your life when you needed guidance, wisdom, a strength beyond yourself? Have you ever been hurting so deeply you needed not just love from God, but clarity and insight? Do I stay married to this person? Do I go ahead and take that job offer? Do I have the surgery? Should I really undergo the treatment? Do I move out of my house? Do I change careers? Do I pursue this relationship? Do I go to this school or that school? Do I invest my money here or there? How should I relate to my child? What should I do about an aging parent? I'm talking about a situation wherein you were forced, I mean practically knocked to the ground because of your circumstances, to turn to God and say, "What should I do? Which way should I go? Show me the way, God, show me the way, please, just a little sign, a little indication, a little blink of a traffic light–right or left, doesn't really matter–just show me the way."

I believe God's spirit leads people. I believe it partly because the tradition of the church says, "Those who are led by the Spirit of God are sons and daughters of God." I believe it partly because men and women throughout the history of faith have testified that it is true. But I also believe it because I have experienced it. And if the polls are correct, most Americans claim they have personally experienced the leading of God in some form or another over the course of their lives.

Sometimes that leading happens by doors going shut or staying shut. Doors I have tried to open with my own brute strength. Doors I have wanted to bulldoze down just so I could get them to open. I have tried, but they have not opened. And when they have not opened, the Spirit of God has helped me to make peace with it. Accept it. We all have closed doors we have to learn to accept. All of us. We all have had doors close that we did not want to close. All of us. But what I have found is that the Spirit has also helped me look for new doors, other doors, different doors to open.

And sometimes that leading has happened by doors opening up. Call it creativity. Call it opportunity. Call it whatever you want to call it, but every now and then I have had this sense of a door opening up, a path being cleared, a cloud lifting and a new clarity being experienced. Now, it still takes courage to walk through the open door. In fact, my sense is that God is opening doors all the time, but we're the ones lacking the courage, the faith, the energy, the commitment to walk through those doors in a positive way. But the doors do open. Sometimes I don't always know if this is the door God wants me to walk through; therefore, I have to learn to discern and listen to the presence of God. In the end, the Spirit of God is all about listening.

To listen to the Spirit is to listen to the deepest voice of life. I like to think of it sometimes as listening to my deepest wisdom. You might want to think of it as listening to your most authentic self. It's the kind of listening that is done with the heart. Not just emotion, but listening with body and mind and soul and spirit. No matter what language you use to describe it, there are those moments when we need guidance, when we have to go deeper, perhaps deeper than we've ever had to go before in order to listen to the Spirit's direction; but if we will listen to the Spirit, the Spirit will speak.

Personally, I think this is what prayer is all about. Prayer is the practice of spiritual alignment. A person might go to the chiropractor because he needs a kind of physical realignment. We take our cars in because the tires need realignment. I pray, in fact, I come to church week after week because I need spiritual realignment. This is not unlike that wonderful line from the movie *Shadowlands,* in which C. S. Lewis says, "I don't pray to change God; I pray to change me." My prayer life begins in silence. I pay attention to my breathing. I quiet my thoughts. I find my peace. I listen. I listen. I listen. And almost always when I pray, almost without fail some wisdom, some direction, some insight and light and calm begins swimming to the surface of my life, like God is a deep-sea diver and slowly, gracefully, beautifully, God swims to the surface, carries me to the surface until we break through and together we experience the light glimmering upon the ocean. It's in the seeing of that light that I often find the guidance I have been missing. I'm aware that what I'm saying cannot be proved in any kind of empirical sense because, in truth, you cannot know this until you try this, you cannot know this unless you are willing to experience this, you cannot know this unless you are willing to see life with a different set of eyes, but in the practice of praying I have found again and again the leading of the Spirit.

Sometimes it's in a door opening, and sometimes closing. At other times it's like allowing a deeper wisdom to surface, but it is all the Spirit of God. I also want to suggest that this process of listening for the Spirit's voice and discerning the opening and closing of doors in life is not an exact science. I know some Christians who speak so glibly about the leading of God, talking about it as if it were an exact science. "God told me to go here. God told me to go there. God told me to turn left or turn right. God told me to shop at this store. Marry this man. Move to this city." Being a Christian and following the lead of the Spirit is not the same as following a city map of Chicago. It's not the same as following a recipe. It's not the same as following a computer manual or architectural blueprints. When it comes to God, there are some mystery and waiting, some mistakes and recovery, some learning and growing, but through it all the Spirit continues to lead.

A lot of times, especially when we're confused or hurt or having to make a hard decision, we pray to God, "Tell me which way I should go." I think we should utter such prayers, but I think more and more the question we need to pray is, "Tell me what kind of person you want me to be." Because where we go is not nearly as important as who we are and who we're trying to become. Will I live today with love? compassion? courage? Will the Spirit inspire me to live today with integrity and authenticity? Will the Spirit move me to be more like Jesus and build human community, creating wholeness in my home, my workplace, my community? This door may shut. That door may open. But in the end, the door that opens or closes is not nearly as important as the kind of person you and I are moment by moment as we walk through our doors in life.

It's true, like most good things in life, I cannot explain the Spirit. Metaphors begin to scratch the surface. Images allow a few rays of light to shine through. Spirit symbols linger in the soul like priceless antique Christmas tree ornaments. But what can be trusted is that there is a spiritual resource, a presence, a spiritual energy living within us that the Spirit builds and pours and guides. To open the heart to that Spirit is to find the ultimate destiny of our humanity; it is to link our hearts with the heart of God.

Postscript

Not long ago a longtime friend came out and asked me, "So, why are you still a Christian? You no longer believe in the literal dimensions of faith, you appreciate other religions, you draw on psychology and literature and poetry for inspiration; why are you even still in the church?"

Well, nothing like an easy question, right?

In a way, this book is my answer.

I am still in the church. I plan to be in the church. I still love the ministry of the church. I still believe in God, Christ, Spirit, church, baptism, eucharist, and the like, the big themes of faith and Christianity. I believe there is a historical foundation to the Christian faith, but the faith must reach beyond history, touching the human heart with love and hope and vitality. I think there is a way to be nurtured by the fundamentals of the faith without being a biblical fundamentalist. I refuse to allow the only Christian voice for our culture to be that of a rigid, conservative, fundamentalist voice. The Christian faith is vibrant and rich, and it can take people places on their spiritual journeys. There is a way to be Christian and keep one's brain and heart intact. There's a way to be a church without being rigid and inflexible. And there's a way to be on a Christian journey and still be in dialogue with other ideas and spiritual resources, with other people and pathways. That's why I stay in the church, and it's why I continue in the ministry.

I would also add that I refuse to accept that the only people passionate about religion are people who have literalized the faith. To put it bluntly—it's about time people who are open and accepting become passionate about the energy of God they have come to know through Christ. The world needs churches that understand that their call from God is more than self-preservation. It is a call to make a contribution to the human family. To make a difference in the world. To heal the wounds and hurts of people. Churches need to begin exercising courage, not by standing up for their beliefs but, like Jesus, standing up for people who are scurrying and scrambling, often lost, upon the mountain of existence.

So I offer this book as support for the person inside the church who aches for a larger hope, and for the person outside the church who wonders if there could be a place of welcome within a community of faith. To both there is a resounding yes from God.

There are no endings on the spiritual journey. Passages. Changes. Twists and turns in the road, but no endings. The heart is always opening. Always living with some ache of the Spirit. And likewise the church never arrives. Hope continues to stretch it wider and wider, at least if it is the church called to live the adventure of the Spirit. Think of this book as one little resource for the journey. The journey we share together.

Notes

Introduction

[1]T. S. Eliot, *Four Quartets* (New York: Harcourt Brace Jovanovich, 1943), 59.

[2]Emily Dickinson, as quoted in *The Enlightened Heart*, ed. Stephen Mitchell (New York: HarperCollins, 1989), 114.

[3]Forrest Church, *Lifecraft* (Boston: Beacon Press, 2000), 3.

[4]Rainer Maria Rilke, *Rilke's Book of Hours* (New York: Riverhead, 1996), 59.

Chapter One: Honoring the Religious Heart

[1]Gail Godwin, *Heart* (New York: HarperCollins, 2001), 83–84.

[2]James Carse, *Breakfast at the Victory* (New York: HarperCollins, 1994), 26–27.

[3]Kabir, as quoted in *The Enlightened Heart*, ed. Stephen Mitchell (New York: HarperCollins, 1989), 75.

Chapter Two: It's All about Listening

[1]Parker Palmer, *Let Your Life Speak* (San Francisco: Jóssey-Bass, 2000), 4–5.

[2]Margery Williams, *The Velveteen Rabbit* (Philadelphia: Courage Books, 1984), 6.

Chapter Three: The Weight of Perfection

[1]Henri Nouwen, *The Inner Voice of Love* (New York: Doubleday, 1996), 29.

[2]Reynolds Price, *Feasting the Heart* (New York: Scribner, 2000), 12–14.

Chapter Four: The Heart Aches to Open

[1]Forrest Church, *Life Lines* (Boston: Beacon Press, 1996), 28.

[2]David Gray, "White Ladder" (New York: RCA Records, 2000).

[3]David Wilcox, "Underneath" (Santa Monica, Calif.: Vanguard Records, 1999).

[4]Archibald MacLeish, *J.B.* (Massachusetts: Houghton Mifflin, 1956), 151–53.

Chapter Five: Welcoming the Stranger Home

[1]Mark Gerzon, *Coming Into Our Own* (New York: Delacorte Press, 1992), 115.

[2]George Herbert, as quoted in *The Enlightened Heart*, ed. Stephen Mitchell (New York: HarperCollins, 1989), 84.

[3]Parker Palmer, *Let Your Life Speak* (San Francisco: Jossey-Bass, 2000), 44–46.

[4]Thomas Merton, *New Seeds of Contemplation* (New York: New Directions Publishing, 1961), 31.

[5]Derek Walcott, *Collected Poems 1948–1984* (New York: Noonday Press, 1986), 328.

Chapter Six: The Soul Longs for Healing

[1]Thomas Moore, *Care of the Soul* (New York: HarperCollins, 1992), 19.

[2]Rumi, as quoted in *The Enlightened Heart*, ed. Stephen Mitchell (New York: HarperCollins, 1989), 59.

Chapter Seven: The Power of Hope

[1]Annie Dillard, *For the Time Being* (New York: Random House, 1999), 191.

[2]Thomas Cahill, *The Gifts of the Jews* (New York: Doubleday, 1998), 3–8.

[3]Frederick Buechner, *Wishful Thinking* (New York: Harper & Row, 1973), 29.

Chapter Eight: Respecting the Many Paths

[1]Elaine Prevellet, as quoted in *Nourishing the Soul,* ed. Anne Simpkinson, Charles Simpkinson, and Rose Solari (New York: HarperCollins, 1995), 250.

Chapter Nine: The Human Touch

[1]Annie Dillard, *For the Time Being* (New York: Random House, 1999), 191.

[2]Denise Levertov, *This Great Unknowing* (New York: New Directions Books, 1999), 43.

Chapter 10: The Great Mountain of God

[1]Thomas Merton, *New Seeds of Contemplation* (New York: New Directions Publishing, 1961), 14.

Chapter 11: The Imagination of Compassion

[1]Thomas Merton, *New Seeds of Contemplation* (New York: New Directions Publishing, 1961), 64.

[2]Joseph Cardinal Bernardin, *The Gift of Peace* (Chicago: Loyola Press, 1997), 37–38.

[3]Dalai Lama, as quoted in *Voices from the Heart*, ed. Eddie and Debbie Shapiro (New York: Penguin Putnam, 1998), 3.

Chapter 12: The Wondrous Christ-Burst!

[1]Thomas Merton, *New Seeds of Contemplation* (New York: New Directions Publishing, 1961), 150.

Chapter 13: The Many Faces of Jesus

[1]Jaroslav Pelikan, *Jesus Through the Centuries* (New Haven: Yale University Press, 1985), 1.

[2]Mary Oliver, *New and Selected Poems* (Boston: Beacon Press, 1992), 78–79.

[3]Henri Nouwen, *The Inner Voice of Love* (New York: Doubleday, 1996), 101.

Chapter 14: The Welcome Table of the Spirit

[1]Frederick Buechner, *A Room Called Remember* (New York: Harper & Row, 1984), 18–19.

[2]Harold Kushner, *Who Needs God* (New York: Summit Books, 1989), 181–82.

[3]Garrison Keillor, *Leaving Home* (New York: Viking Penguin, 1987), 1.

Chapter 15: Mapping the Myths

[1]Clark M. Williamson, *Way of Blessing, Way of Life* (St. Louis: Chalice Press, 1999), 97.

Chapter 16: The Divine Dialogue

[1]John B. Cobb, Jr., *Becoming a Thinking Christian* (Nashville: Abingdon Press, 1993), 8.

[2]*Adventures of the Mind,* ed. Richard Thurelsen and John Kobler (New York: Curtis Publishing, 1959).

Chapter 17: The Crucible of the Church

[1]Anne Lamott, *Traveling Mercies* (New York: Random House, 1999), 100.

[2]Ibid., 63–65.

[3]Ignazio Silone, *Bread and Wine* (New York: New American Library, 1963), 268.

[4]Nora Gallagher, *Things Seen and Unseen* (New York: Alfred A. Knopf, 1998), 11–13.

[5]Henri Nouwen, *The Inner Voice of Love* (New York: Doubleday, 1996), 81.

Chapter 18: Resources of the Spirit

[1]Pierre Teilhard de Chardin, *Hymn of the Universe* (New York: Harper Torchbooks, 1961), 29.